GAMES

FROM

CHILDHOOD

GAMES
FROM
CHILDHOOD

A NOSTALGIC COMPENDIUM OF GAMES WE USED TO PLAY

Compiled and edited
by Karen Dolby

Michael O'Mara Books Limited

First published in Great Britain in 2017 by
Michael O'Mara Books Limited
9 Lion Yard
Tremadoc Road
London SW4 7NQ

A CIP catalogue record for this book is available from the British Library.

Papers used by Michael O'Mara Books Limited are natural, recyclable products
made from wood grown in sustainable forests. The manufacturing processes
conform to the environmental regulations of the country of origin.

ISBN: 978-1-78243-721-5 in paperback
ISBN: 978-1-78243-825-0 in hardback

1 2 3 4 5 6 7 8 9 10

Designed by Ana Bjezancevic and Jade Wheaton

Illustrations: shutterstock.com

Printed in China

www.mombooks.com

Introduction

What a complicated world we live in. Computer screens blink at us at every turn and mobile phones demand our attention twenty-four hours a day. At first it was thought that the internet would liberate us from the tedious things in life, freeing more time for leisure and what makes us truly happy. Of course, we now know that constantly being available can be something of a tyranny.

Recently, there has been a backlash and a realization of some of the things that have perhaps been lost over these computer decades. 'Digital detox' is the new buzz phrase: people are turning away from their phones and tablets, embracing the old ways. Sales of vinyl records are flourishing. The must-have Christmas present is a traditional board game. Fountain pens and good old-fashioned 'sharpies' are finding their way back into people's hands. Drawing and painting materials are again selling well in shops and online. We want to bake and paint and reclaim how we spend time in our own way.

Alongside this, we are rediscovering the joys of simple, traditional pen and paper games like Hangman and Noughts and Crosses. They are fun to play, and perfect for holidays, journeys, spare moments, or when the battery is dead on the iPad or phone. They are social activities. They can be played with family and friends of any age and are a terrific way to break the ice in groups or at parties. Games can be funny or challenging, testing knowledge or strategy skills. They can be used as teaching tools and are an important part of socialization, encouraging bonding and introducing the notions of rules, agreed aims, competition and the element of chance. They have a fascinating history and have always been an essential part of the development of culture, reflecting our human capacity for imagination.

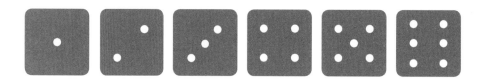

Games were considered important enough to be included among the treasures entombed with Egyptian pharaohs. Backgammon, Draughts and Chess are known to date back millennia but so do games such as Noughts and Crosses and Nine Men's Morris. Archaeologists have uncovered carved boards for these three-in-a-row-type games throughout Ancient Rome. Word puzzles were also popular and the same word square has been discovered engraved in the ruins of Pompeii as well as in Roman cities around the world. Known as the SATOR acrostic, this simple word poem might have held a secret significance, helping persecuted Christians to identify one another.

The same games, or recognizable versions of them, are surprisingly widespread. Nine Men's Morris is played throughout Europe, Russia, Northern Africa and Asia, perhaps spread by Viking raiders as they sailed the globe. Dots and Boxes is another game that is known throughout Europe and Scandinavia, with versions played in South America.

All the games included in this book have been passed on from generation to generation, by word of mouth and example. They can be played anywhere, anytime and in most cases need nothing more than a pencil or pen and a willing opponent. Many people will have fond memories of playing them as children. I still recall hotly contested wet playtime games of Hangman. And I can well remember the moment the penny finally dropped and I realized that I had a far better chance of winning Noughts and Crosses if I began in one of the corners.

Games from Childhood contains firm favourites alongside those that may be less well known. All can be made to work at any level from the simplest to the most challenging. You will find clear instructions, tips on strategy, printed grids to use, as well as ideas for useful subjects and words. These are intended to be a starting point to encourage other ideas. The joy of these games is that you can make them your own and be as personal and creative with them as you like.

BATTLESHIPS

The strategic guessing game for two players, Battleships is thought to date back to World War I and a French game called 'L'Attaque', although it possibly goes back further to the nineteenth century and may have been played by Russian military officers.

Whatever its origins, the board game has remained popular and widely played since the first commercial edition, called 'Salvo', was sold in the US, in 1931. Others quickly followed and in 1967, the Milton Bradley games company produced a version using plastic boards, pegs and ships. There are now electronic and computer spin-offs, including one called 'Battleship Islands', which features captured figures. In 2012, the game even inspired a film.

The game is very easy to play on paper grids, typically a square of ten rows of ten with the side lines marked A to J and the top lines labelled 1 to 10, and five ships for each player, although grid sizes along with numbers and types of ships used can vary. Different countries also tend to have their own specifications and quirks.

RULES OF THE GAME

According to the Milton Bradley rules for the game, the ships are in descending size order:

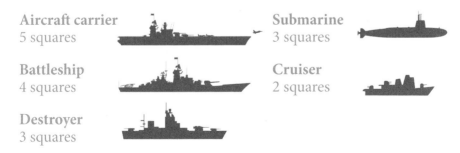

Aircraft carrier
5 squares

Battleship
4 squares

Destroyer
3 squares

Submarine
3 squares

Cruiser
2 squares

- Each player draws their ships on their fleet grid –'My Ships'– in secret. The ships can be positioned anywhere on the grid but must go horizontally or vertically, never on a diagonal, and none must overlap.

- Players also each have a tracking grid –'Enemy Ships'– on which to mark their shots.

- Players then take turns to fire at their opponent's ships. In each round the attacker identifies the square they are aiming at, marking the shot on their tracking grid. Their opponent must say whether the shot has found a target and mark the shot on their fleet grid. On both grids, hits are recorded with an O and misses with an X.

- When every square of a ship has been hit, the player announces that it has been sunk.

- The game's winner is the first person to sink all of their opponent's ships.

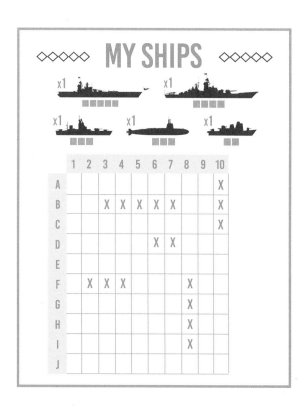

PLAYER 1

ENEMY SHIPS

	1	2	3	4	5	6	7	8	9	10
A										
B										
C										
D										
E										
F										
G										
H										
I										
J										

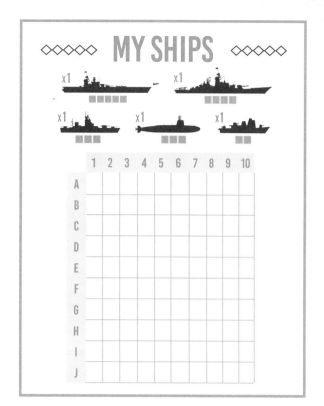

PLAYER 2

ENEMY SHIPS

	1	2	3	4	5	6	7	8	9	10
A										
B										
C										
D										
E										
F										
G										
H										
I										
J										

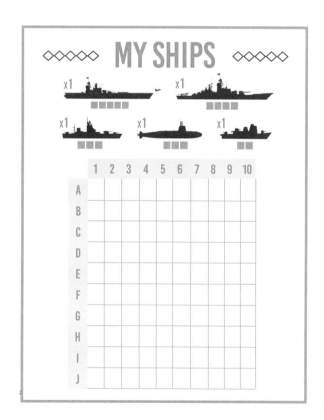

PLAYER 1

ENEMY SHIPS

	1	2	3	4	5	6	7	8	9	10
A										
B										
C										
D										
E										
F										
G										
H										
I										
J										

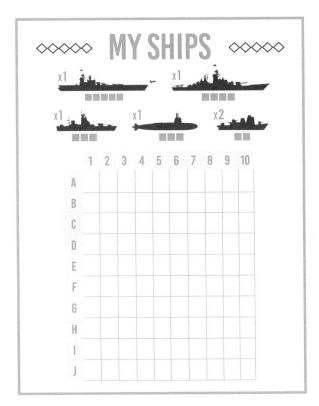

PLAYER 2

ENEMY SHIPS

	1	2	3	4	5	6	7	8	9	10
A										
B										
C										
D										
E										
F										
G										
H										
I										
J										

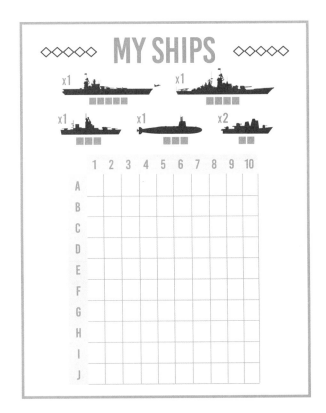

PLAYER 1

ENEMY SHIPS

	1	2	3	4	5	6	7	8	9	10
A										
B										
C										
D										
E										
F										
G										
H										
I										
J										

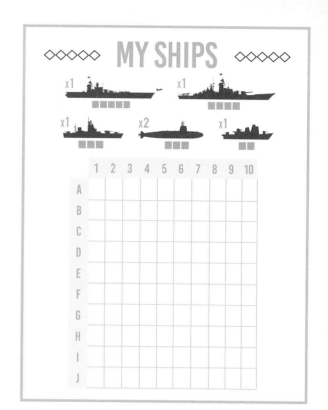

MY SHIPS

	1	2	3	4	5	6	7	8	9	10
A										
B										
C										
D										
E										
F										
G										
H										
I										
J										

PLAYER 2

ENEMY SHIPS

	1	2	3	4	5	6	7	8	9	10
A										
B										
C										
D										
E										
F										
G										
H										
I										
J										

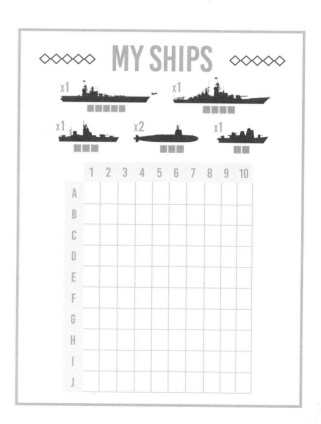

MY SHIPS

	1	2	3	4	5	6	7	8	9	10
A										
B										
C										
D										
E										
F										
G										
H										
I										
J										

PLAYER 1

ENEMY SHIPS

	1	2	3	4	5	6	7	8	9	10
A										
B										
C										
D										
E										
F										
G										
H										
I										
J										

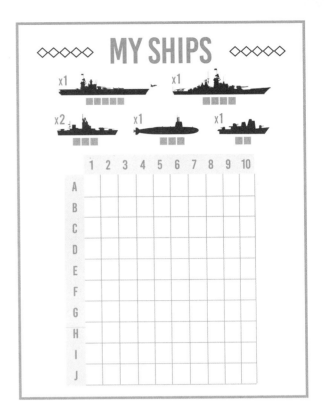

PLAYER 2

ENEMY SHIPS

	1	2	3	4	5	6	7	8	9	10
A										
B										
C										
D										
E										
F										
G										
H										
I										
J										

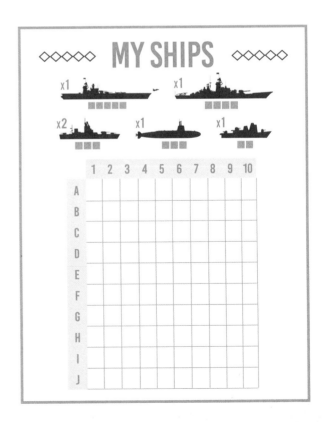

PLAYER 1

ENEMY SHIPS

	1	2	3	4	5	6	7	8	9	10
A										
B										
C										
D										
E										
F										
G										
H										
I										
J										

PLAYER 2

ENEMY SHIPS

	1	2	3	4	5	6	7	8	9	10
A										
B										
C										
D										
E										
F										
G										
H										
I										
J										

PLAYER 1

ENEMY SHIPS

	1	2	3	4	5	6	7	8	9	10
A										
B										
C										
D										
E										
F										
G										
H										
I										
J										

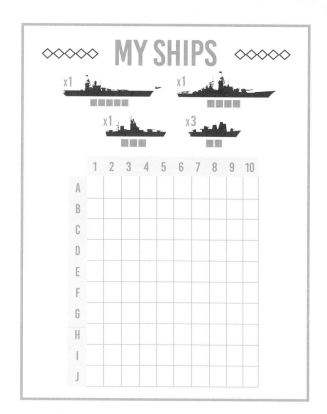

PLAYER 2

ENEMY SHIPS

	1	2	3	4	5	6	7	8	9	10
A										
B										
C										
D										
E										
F										
G										
H										
I										
J										

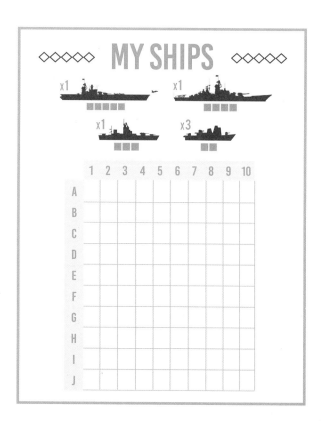

ENEMY SHIPS

	1	2	3	4	5	6	7	8	9	10	11	12
A												
B												
C												
D												
E												
F												
G												
H												
I												
J												
K												
L												

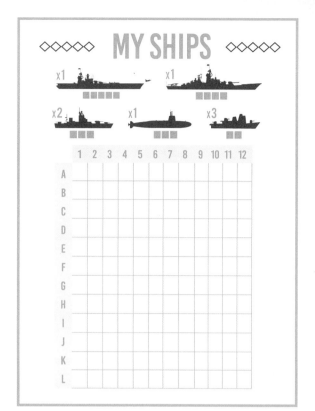

PLAYER 2

ENEMY SHIPS

	1	2	3	4	5	6	7	8	9	10	11	12
A												
B												
C												
D												
E												
F												
G												
H												
I												
J												
K												
L												

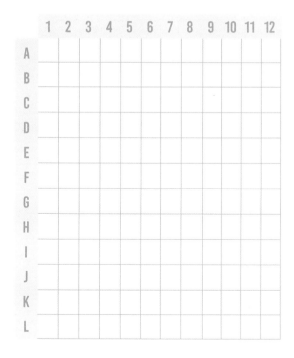

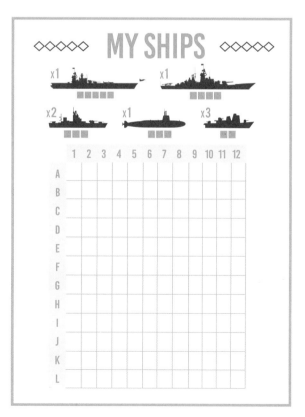

PLAYER 1

ENEMY SHIPS

	1	2	3	4	5	6	7	8	9	10	11	12
A												
B												
C												
D												
E												
F												
G												
H												
I												
J												
K												
L												

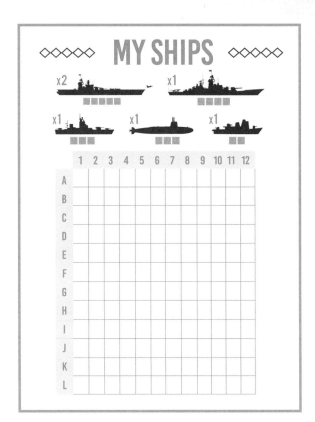

MY SHIPS

	1	2	3	4	5	6	7	8	9	10	11	12
A												
B												
C												
D												
E												
F												
G												
H												
I												
J												
K												
L												

PLAYER 2

ENEMY SHIPS

	1	2	3	4	5	6	7	8	9	10	11	12
A												
B												
C												
D												
E												
F												
G												
H												
I												
J												
K												
L												

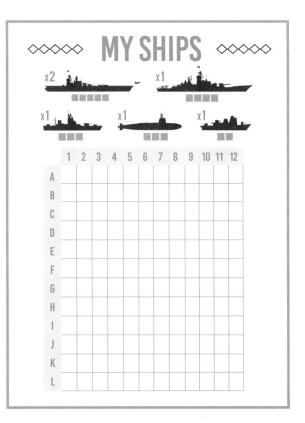

MY SHIPS

	1	2	3	4	5	6	7	8	9	10	11	12
A												
B												
C												
D												
E												
F												
G												
H												
I												
J												
K												
L												

 **PLAYER 1**

ENEMY SHIPS

	1	2	3	4	5	6	7	8	9	10	11	12
A												
B												
C												
D												
E												
F												
G												
H												
I												
J												
K												
L												

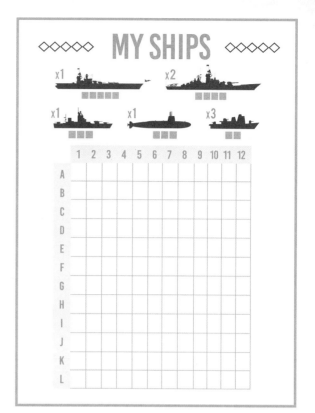

MY SHIPS

x1 x2 x1 x1 x3

	1	2	3	4	5	6	7	8	9	10	11	12
A												
B												
C												
D												
E												
F												
G												
H												
I												
J												
K												
L												

PLAYER 2

ENEMY SHIPS

	1	2	3	4	5	6	7	8	9	10	11	12
A												
B												
C												
D												
E												
F												
G												
H												
I												
J												
K												
L												

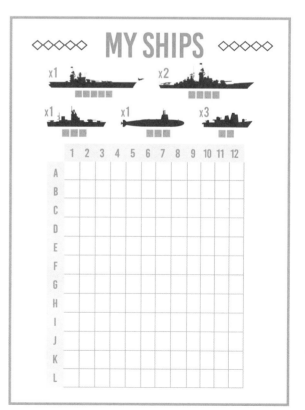

MY SHIPS

x1 x2 x1 x1 x3

	1	2	3	4	5	6	7	8	9	10	11	12
A												
B												
C												
D												
E												
F												
G												
H												
I												
J												
K												
L												

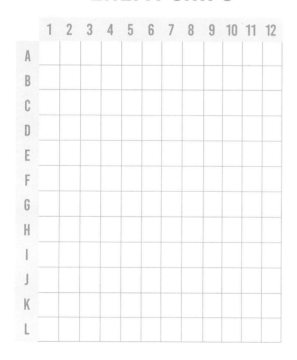

PLAYER 1

ENEMY SHIPS

	1	2	3	4	5	6	7	8	9	10	11	12
A												
B												
C												
D												
E												
F												
G												
H												
I												
J												
K												
L												

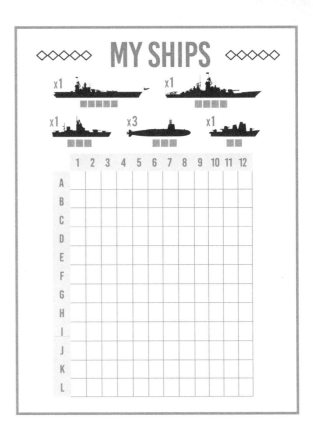

MY SHIPS

	1	2	3	4	5	6	7	8	9	10	11	12
A												
B												
C												
D												
E												
F												
G												
H												
I												
J												
K												
L												

PLAYER 2

ENEMY SHIPS

	1	2	3	4	5	6	7	8	9	10	11	12
A												
B												
C												
D												
E												
F												
G												
H												
I												
J												
K												
L												

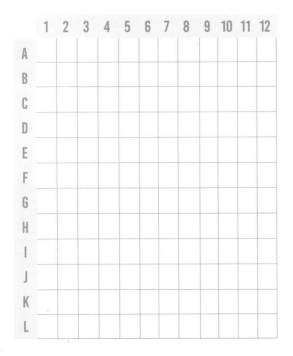

MY SHIPS

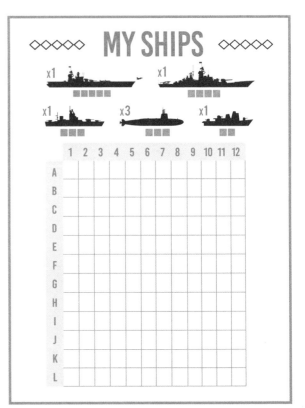

	1	2	3	4	5	6	7	8	9	10	11	12
A												
B												
C												
D												
E												
F												
G												
H												
I												
J												
K												
L												

ENEMY SHIPS

	1	2	3	4	5	6	7	8	9	10	11	12
A												
B												
C												
D												
E												
F												
G												
H												
I												
J												
K												
L												

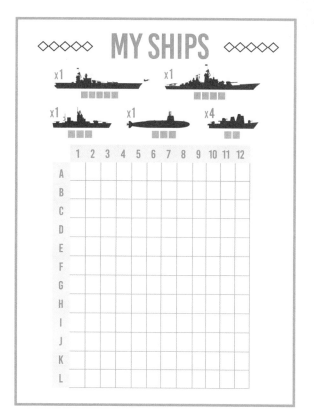

MY SHIPS

	1	2	3	4	5	6	7	8	9	10	11	12
A												
B												
C												
D												
E												
F												
G												
H												
I												
J												
K												
L												

PLAYER 2

ENEMY SHIPS

	1	2	3	4	5	6	7	8	9	10	11	12
A												
B												
C												
D												
E												
F												
G												
H												
I												
J												
K												
L												

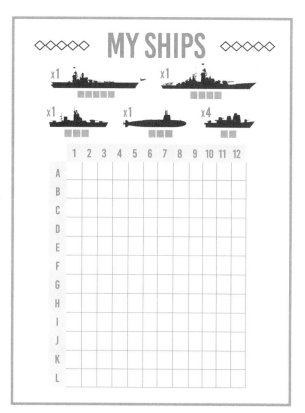

MY SHIPS

	1	2	3	4	5	6	7	8	9	10	11	12
A												
B												
C												
D												
E												
F												
G												
H												
I												
J												
K												
L												

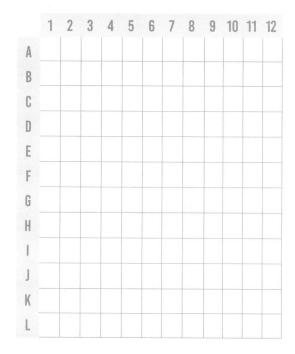

PLAYER 1

ENEMY SHIPS

	1	2	3	4	5	6	7	8	9	10	11	12
A												
B												
C												
D												
E												
F												
G												
H												
I												
J												
K												
L												

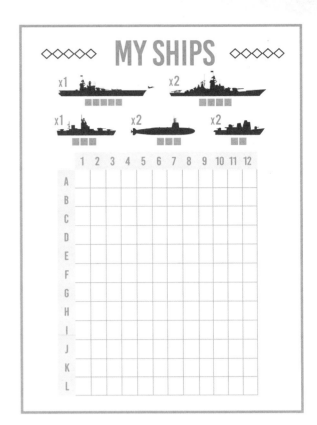

PLAYER 2

ENEMY SHIPS

	1	2	3	4	5	6	7	8	9	10	11	12
A												
B												
C												
D												
E												
F												
G												
H												
I												
J												
K												
L												

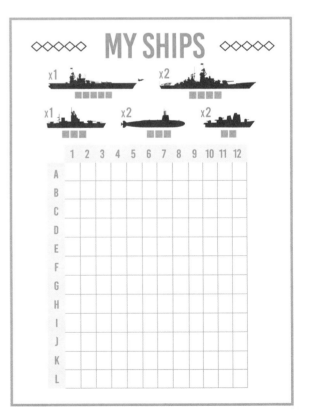

HANGMAN

This used to be a staple of wet playtimes at primary schools and is sometimes called 'Gallows' or the 'Game of Hanging'. It was already known as a traditional game in Victorian times, although it was then referred to as 'Birds, Beasts and Fishes' by Alice Bertha Gomme, a folklorist who made a study of children's games at the end of the nineteenth century.

Hangman is a satisfying word game that can also be a useful tool for practising language and improving vocabulary. In recent years, concerns have been voiced about just how appropriate it is to use gallows as a symbol, especially for children. Schoolteachers often get round this by instead drawing the outline of a tree with ten apples that can then be coloured in as guesses are used up.

RULES OF THE GAME

Hangman needs at least two players. The first player thinks of a word or phrase and draws a number of dashes to represent each letter.

The aim of the game is basically to guess the word or phrase before your man gets hanged.

Every correct letter guessed is marked in the right place on the row of dashes as many times as it appears, but if the guesser gets it wrong, a line is drawn in on the hangman's gallows. At any point, the guessing player may make a calculated suggestion for the whole word. If correct, this wins the game; if wrong, a penalty line is drawn and the noose tightens.

The executioner can choose to be kind by offering a clue at any point.

The number of incorrect guesses possible is up to individual players. In some versions of the game, the gallows are already drawn and only the hanging figure must be completed. In others, extra lines are added to the gallows and sometimes a face is included on the figure.

In all versions, the winner is the first to finish. The guesser wins if he completes the word before the diagram is complete, and the player setting the puzzle wins if he completes the hangman before his opponent works out the word. If you have more than one guesser, take turns and make sure each guesser uses their own hangman. The winner chooses the word for the next game.

The word choice can be left open but the game can be made more interesting by choosing from categories specialized enough to test in-depth knowledge of a subject. Phrases or sentences can also be chosen so that song, film or book titles and quotations can be used to challenge opponents.

 TIP

Try to remember the acronym ETAOIN SHRDLU. True, it's almost impossible to pronounce, but it shows the order of the most frequently occurring letters in English. Finding words that include few of these twelve letters will boost your chances of winning.

Ideas for Hangman categories

Animals	Names – female,	Oscar winners
Cat species	male or surnames	Song titles
Dog breeds		
Famous cats and dogs	Capital cities	TV series
Fish	Chemistry	
Reptiles	Countries	Book titles
Birds	Gemstones	Heroes and heroines
	Rivers	
Adjectives	US states	Sport
Nouns		Football teams
Verbs	Actors and actresses	Tennis champions
Collective nouns	Film titles	Olympic medal holders

6-LETTER WORD

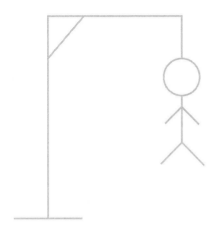

_ _ _ _ _ _

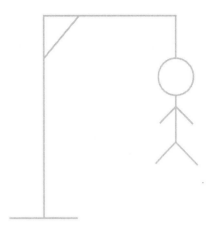

_ _ _ _ _ _

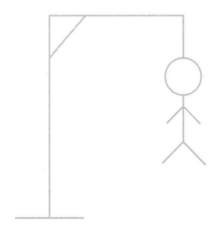

_ _ _ _ _ _

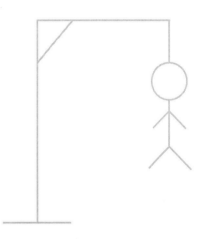

_ _ _ _ _ _

USED LETTERS			
PLAYER 1	PLAYER 2	PLAYER 3	PLAYER 4

6-LETTER WORD

- - - - - -

- - - - - -

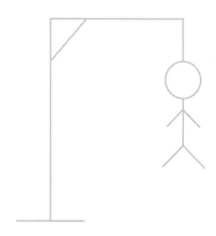

- - - - - -

- - - - - -

USED LETTERS			
PLAYER 1	PLAYER 2	PLAYER 3	PLAYER 4

7-LETTER WORD

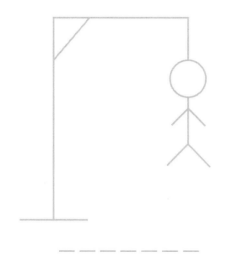

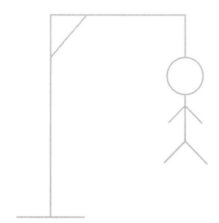

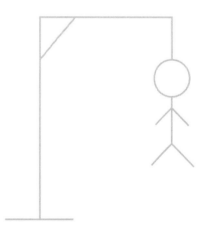

USED LETTERS			
PLAYER 1	PLAYER 2	PLAYER 3	PLAYER 4

7-LETTER WORD

USED LETTERS			
PLAYER 1	PLAYER 2	PLAYER 3	PLAYER 4

8-LETTER WORD

USED LETTERS			
PLAYER 1	PLAYER 2	PLAYER 3	PLAYER 4

9-LETTER WORD

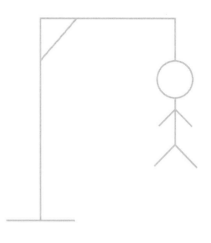

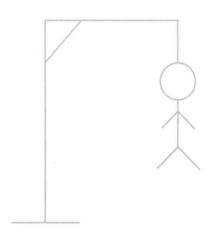

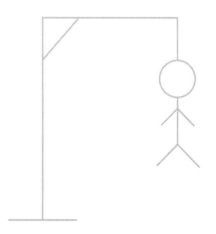

USED LETTERS			
PLAYER 1	PLAYER 2	PLAYER 3	PLAYER 4

10-LETTER WORD

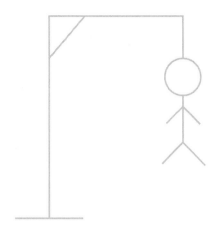

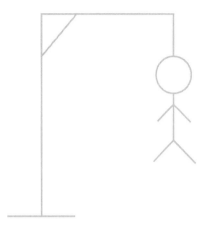

- - - - - - - - - -

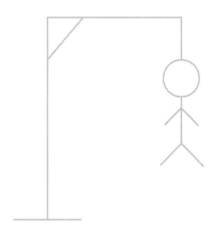

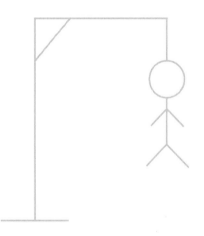

- - - - - - - - - -

USED LETTERS			
PLAYER 1	PLAYER 2	PLAYER 3	PLAYER 4

11- & 12-LETTER WORD

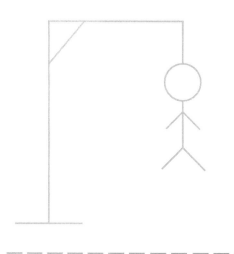

USED LETTERS			
PLAYER 1	PLAYER 2	PLAYER 3	PLAYER 4

13- & 14-LETTER WORD

– – – – – – – – – – – – – –

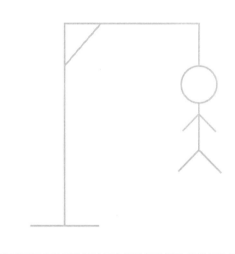

– – – – – – – – – – – – – –

USED LETTERS			
PLAYER 1	PLAYER 2	PLAYER 3	PLAYER 4

UP TO YOU!

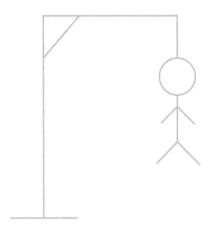

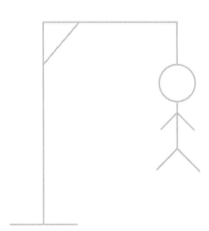

USED LETTERS			
PLAYER 1	PLAYER 2	PLAYER 3	PLAYER 4

Word wise

Here are a few ideas for words of varying lengths.

Six letters

Abject
Empire
Lagoon
Manage
Muzzle
Orange
Vicious
Pajama

Seven letters

Anxiety
Dynamic
Jacuzzi
Neutral
Obscure
Rhodium
Phoenix
Whizzed

Eight letters

Analysis
Blizzard
Doubtful
Mnemonic
Flapjack
Friendly
Strength
Yachting

Nine letters

Chocolate
Education
Kickboxer
Maximized
Necessary
Nocturnal
Rotavator
Xylophone

Ten letters

Aberration
Gobsmacked
Gondoliers
Helicopter
Liberality
Somersault
Tobogganed
Waterproof

Eleven letters

Adolescence
Bourgeoisie
Gravitation
Lamplighter
Mountaineer
Nucleotides
Obnoxiously
Squirrelled

Twelve letters

Accentuating
Backflipping
Bedazzlement
Cryptography
Frustrations
Kaleidoscope
Lexicography
Misanthropic
Quixotically
Reconcilable
Scrupulously
Tranquilizer
Urbanization

Thirteen letters

Advertisement
Brainstorming
Characterisms
Dysfunctional
Extraordinary
Fruitarianism
Gerrymanderer
Hydrogenation
Postmodernism
Questionnaire
Unimaginative
Zoopsychology

And for the truly long-winded:

Sesquipedalian – 14

Incomprehensibilities – 21

Honorificabilitudinitatibus – 27
(the longest word in Shakespeare; also alternates consonants and vowels)

Antidisestablishmentarianism – 28

Supercalifragilisticexpialidocious – 34

The longest isograms, i.e. words that do not repeat any letters, are:
Subdermatoglyphic and Uncopyrightable

In case you're wondering, the longest word in English is a whopping forty-five letters:

Pneumonoultramicroscopicsilicovolcanoconiosis.

Like many of the other most lengthy words in the dictionary it is a medical term, and the name for a lung disease caused by inhalation of silica or quartz dust.

Also good for confusing opponents are words that don't contain any vowels, as most people try to guess vowels first:

Crypt

Cwtch

Flyby

Gypsy

Hymn

Lynch

Lynx

Myrrh

Myth

Psych

Pygmy

Rhythm

Sphynx

Spryly

Sylph

Tsktsks (the expression of annoyance and the longest vowel-less word in the English language)

Tryst

Categories

This easy-to-play word game can be as challenging as you want. It works best with at least three players and really, the more the merrier if you want a serious competition. So called because players have to think of words in a chosen category that begin with certain letters, Categories is popular in many countries.

The game is also sometimes known as Guggenheim, possibly because it was a favourite of the Guggenheim family at the beginning of the twentieth century. The American journalist Frank Scully, who more famously wrote about UFOs and flying saucers, also published a series of books on games for convalescents called *Fun in Bed* in which he suggested a different reason for the name.

Scully's story has it that P. G. Wodehouse, Jerome Kern and Howard Dietz were playing Categories when Kern wrote down Gutenberg as the name of a printer. Wodehouse had never heard of the Gutenberg printing press and refused to believe this was a real name. When another round of the game was suggested some months later, Wodehouse agreed but on the condition, 'no more of your Guggenheims'. Believe it or not, the name stuck.

RULES OF THE GAME

Five categories are chosen and each player writes them down the left-hand side of their paper. Here are some suggestions for possibilities but categories can be almost anything, depending on who's playing.

Choose your category

Actors	Emotions	Musical instruments
Animals	Film	Names
Art	Fish	Occupations
Authors	Flowers	Oscar winners
Birds	Food and drink	Planets
Capitals	Football	Plants
Cars	Fruit	Poets
Cinema	Geography	Presidents
Cities	History	Reptiles
Colours	Machines	Sports
Countries	Minerals	Vegetables

Next, players pick a keyword, which is written across the top of the paper. Again, any word can be chosen but ideally it should be five or six letters long with no repeated letters. Any keywords containing Q, X and Z would pose an almost impossible challenge for most players and even the letters K and Y can be tricky. Suggestions are printed below:

Amuse	Ocean	Player
Games	Flower	Tricky
House	Knight	Quick
Night	Pencil	Yacht

Taking each letter of the keyword as the initial, players then have to think of a word for all five categories.

It is usual to set a time limit of five to ten minutes. At the end of the round answers are compared. A player scores a point for each other player who does not have the same word, so if five people are playing and only two have come up with a particular word, they would each score three points for it. Points are counted at the end and the winner is the player with the highest score.

Categories

Keyword Categories	T	R	I	C	K	Y	Score
COLOUR	TAUPE	RED	INDIGO	CERISE	KHAKI	YELLOW	
PLACE	TORONTO	ROME	IRELAND	CHICAGO	KENTUCKY	YORK	
NAME	TIM	RYAN	ISOBEL	CHRISTINE	KATE	YVETTE	
ANIMAL	TIGER	REINDEER	IGUANA	CAT	KANGAROO	YETI	
SOMETHING YOU WEAR	TIGHTS	ROBE	ICE SKATES	CAP	KILT	Y-FRONTS	
Total							

CATEGORIES

Keyword

Categories

Total

Score

Categories

Keyword Categories					Score
					Total

CATEGORIES

Keyword

Categories

Total

Score

Categories

Keyword Categories						Score
						Total

CATEGORIES

Keyword Categories						Total
						Score

Categories

Keyword

Categories

Keyword Categories						Score
						Total

❖ ♣ CATEGORIES ♣ ❖

Keyword Categories						Score
Total						

Categories

Score

Total

Keyword

Categories

CATEGORIES

Keyword
Categories

Total

Score

Categories

Keyword Categories						Score
						Total

◆◆◆◆ Categories ◆◆◆◆

Keyword Categories					Score
Total					

CROSSED WORDS

This more taxing version of a conventional crossword will keep your brain ticking over nicely and provide you and your opponent with a mighty challenge. There's also a hint of Scrabble about it as you struggle to create words from a diminishing supply of letters.

The crossword puzzle itself may be one of the most widely popular word games in the world but it's not actually that old. The first crossword was printed in the US newspaper *New York World* in December 1913 and was the work of Arthur Wynne, a Liverpudlian journalist who emigrated to New York. The idea quickly caught on.

RULES OF THE GAME

- The rules are fairly simple. Each grid is accompanied by the twenty-six letters of the alphabet, printed in a row above it and below it.

- Player One chooses a word and writes it on the grid, crossing out all the letters used from the top alphabet.

- Player Two then adds a word to the first word on the grid, crossing out all the new letters used from the bottom alphabet. The letter used from the first word is not crossed out.

- Players then take turns to add to the words on the grid using the available letters left in their alphabets.

RULES THAT CANNOT BE BROKEN:

- No player can use a letter more than once, so when a letter has been crossed out it cannot be played again.

- Words can run horizontally from left to right and vertically from top to bottom, but they cannot go side by side unless any pairs of letters created also make new words.

- The game is over when neither player is able to make any more words from their leftover alphabet.

- The winner is the player who has used the most letters.

 TIP

It can be helpful if both players use a different colour pen or Player One uses capital letters and Player Two uses lower case.

A B C D E F G H I J K L M N O P Q R S T U V W X Y Z

							B	o	u	g	h				
							U								
							S								
					C	i	t	y							
					H										
			s	k	I	d									
			N		L										
		b	o	I	D										
			W												
P	R	A	Y												
r															
a															
n	E	X	T												
c															
e															

a b c d e f g h i j k l m n o p q r s t u v w x y z

CROSSED WORDS

A B C D E F G H I J K L M N O P Q R S T U V W X Y Z

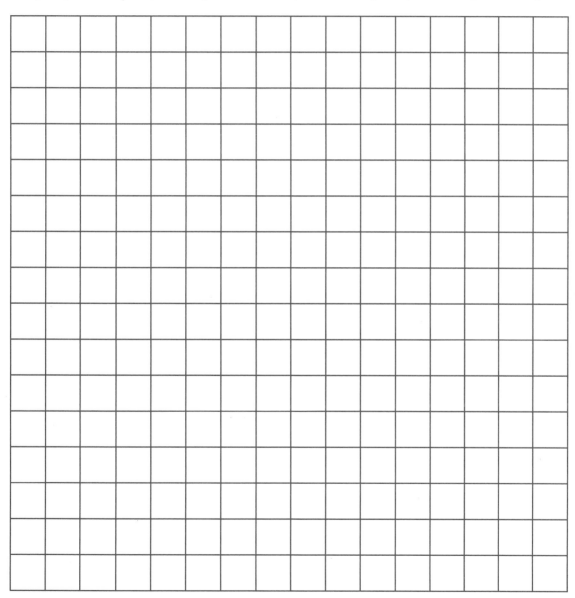

a b c d e f g h i j k l m n o p q r s t u v w x y z

A B C D E F G H I J K L M N O P Q R S T U V W X Y Z

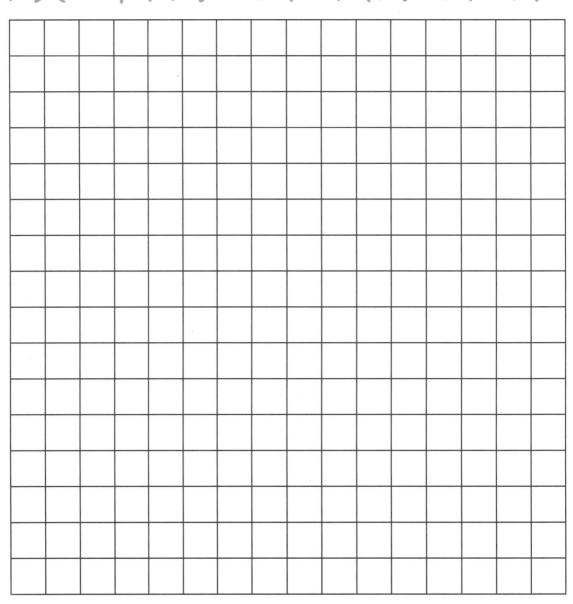

a b c d e f g h i j k l m n o p q r s t u v w x y z

CROSSED WORDS

A B C D E F G H I J K L M N O P Q R S T U V W X Y Z

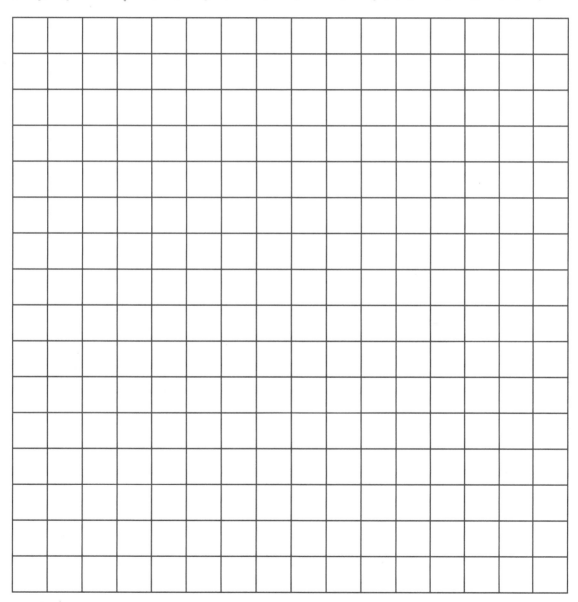

a b c d e f g h i j k l m n o p q r s t u v w x y z

CROSSED WORDS

ABCDEFGHIJKLMNOPQRSTUVWXYZ

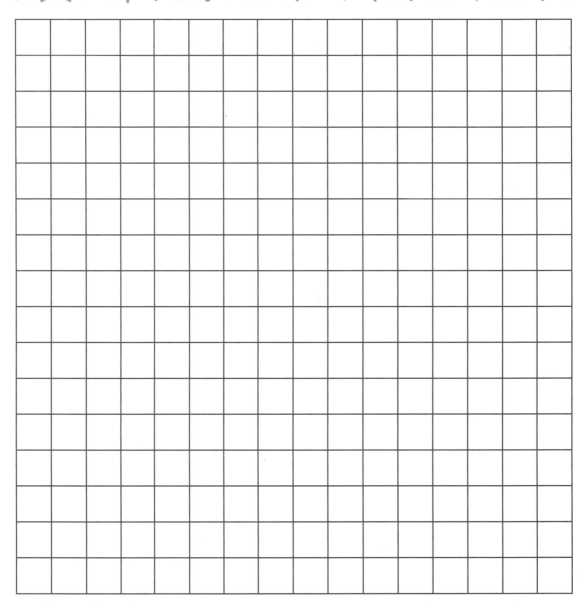

abcdefghijklmnopqrstuvwxyz

A B C D E F G H I J K L M N O P Q R S T U V W X Y Z

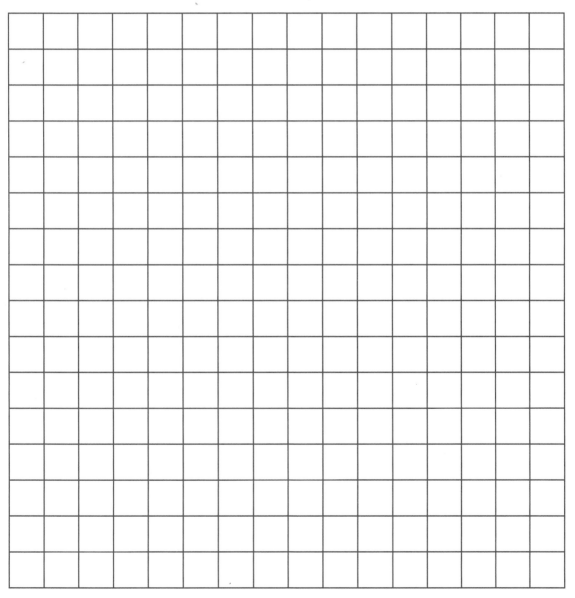

a b c d e f g h i j k l m n o p q r s t u v w x y z

CROSSED WORDS

A B C D E F G H I J K L M N O P Q R S T U V W X Y Z

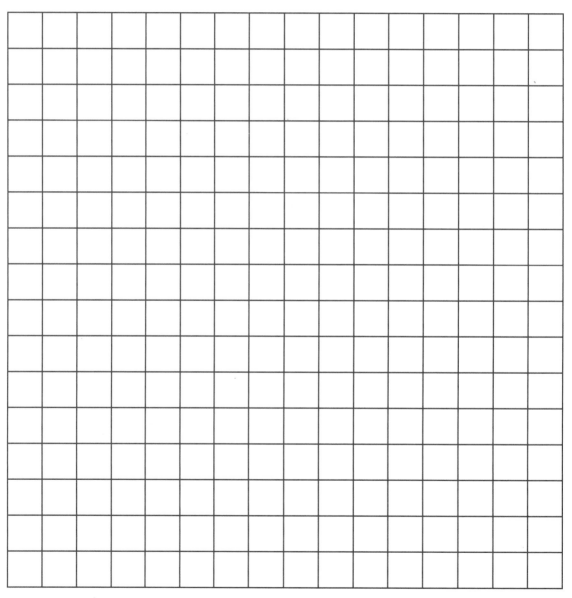

a b c d e f g h i j k l m n o p q r s t u v w x y z

CROSSED WORDS

A B C D E F G H I J K L M N O P Q R S T U V W X Y Z

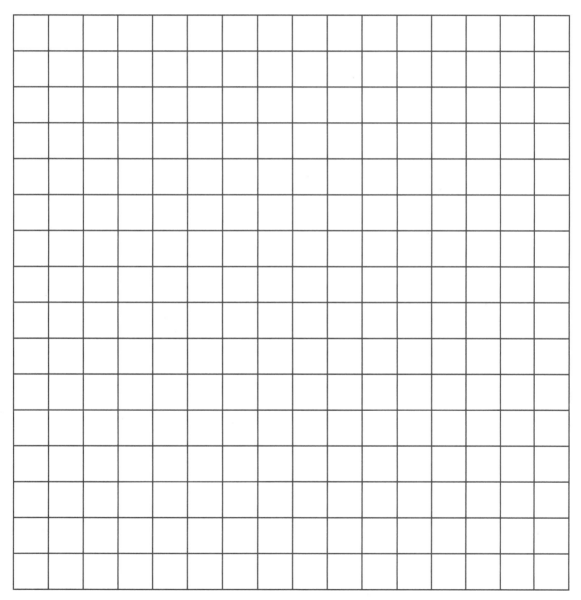

a b c d e f g h i j k l m n o p q r s t u v w x y z

CROSSED WORDS

A B C D E F G H I J K L M N O P Q R S T U V W X Y Z

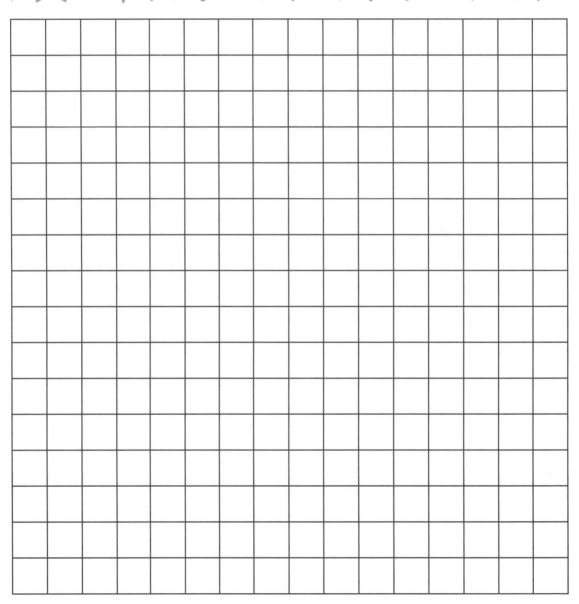

a b c d e f g h i j k l m n o p q r s t u v w x y z

A B C D E F G H I J K L M N O P Q R S T U V W X Y Z

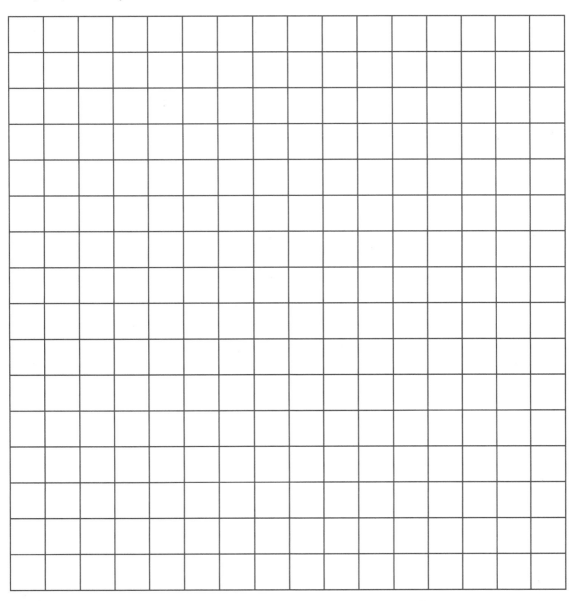

a b c d e f g h i j k l m n o p q r s t u v w x y z

CROSSED WORDS

A B C D E F G H I J K L M N O P Q R S T U V W X Y Z

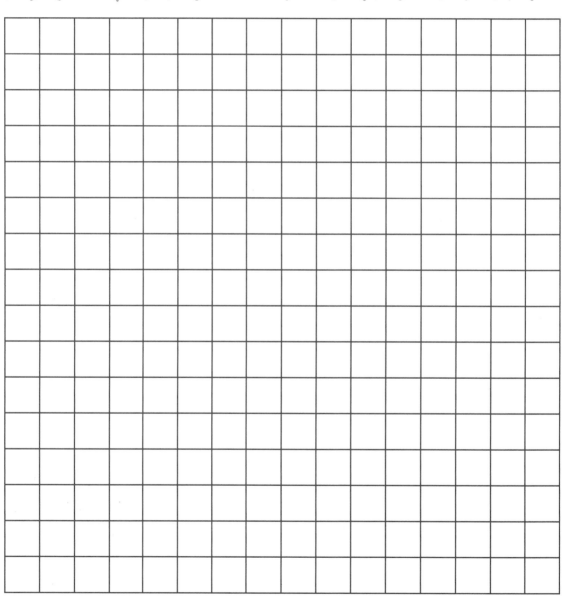

a b c d e f g h i j k l m n o p q r s t u v w x y z

CROSSED WORDS

A B C D E F G H I J K L M N O P Q R S T U V W X Y Z

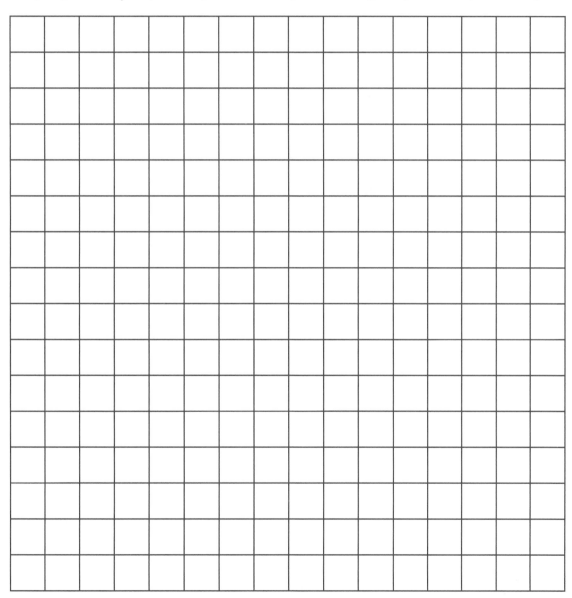

a b c d e f g h i j k l m n o p q r s t u v w x y z

A B C D E F G H I J K L M N O P Q R S T U V W X Y Z

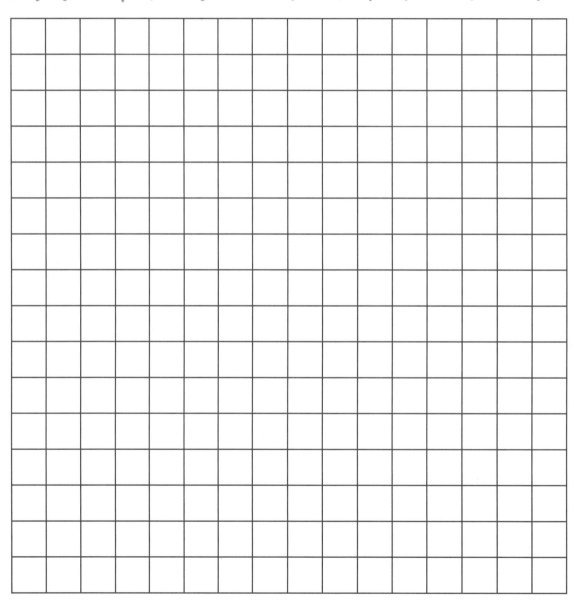

a b c d e f g h i j k l m n o p q r s t u v w x y z

~ Noughts and Crosses ~

Is there anyone who has never played Noughts and Crosses? This most traditional of all traditional games has been a firm favourite for generations. In fact, versions of the game have been popular since classical times and archaeologists have even uncovered grid markings in Ancient Rome. During the first century BC it was known as *Terni Lapilli* and the game has been called various names, most often Noughts and Crosses in Britain and Tic Tac Toe in the US, possibly from a sixteenth-century version of backgammon called 'Tick-tack'.

The pencil and paper game is played on a grid of nine squares, arranged in three rows of three. Although simple, it is estimated there are almost 20,000 possible layouts and successful players use strategy and observation to win.

RULES OF THE GAME

- This is a game for two players.

- Players use either Os or Xs. The first player marks their O or X in any of the squares on the grid. Player two follows, choosing any of the other spaces. The players then take turns, trying to make a straight line of noughts or crosses while blocking their opponent's attempts to do the same.

- The winner is the first player to make a straight line of three noughts or crosses in a row, horizontally, vertically or diagonally.

- If no one succeeds when the grid is full, the game is a tie.

TIP

The player who goes first has a definite advantage.
The best start is to choose a corner square, in which case
the best defence for the next player is to opt for the centre.

∿ Super Noughts and Crosses ∿

This scaled-up version of the game has slightly different rules and can last longer. Player 1 is Crosses and places one cross each time. Player 2 is Noughts and places two noughts each time. Noughts is trying to get five in a row; Crosses is trying to block them and fill the board. Player One (crosses) begins. The game ends when Noughts gets five in a row or the board is filled.

Example 1　　　　　**Example 2**

O X O X O O O X O O X X O O X O X X O O O O O X O	O · · X O O · X O O X X O O O · X O O O O X X O

Player 1 wins　　　　**Player 2 wins**

~ Noughts and Crosses ~

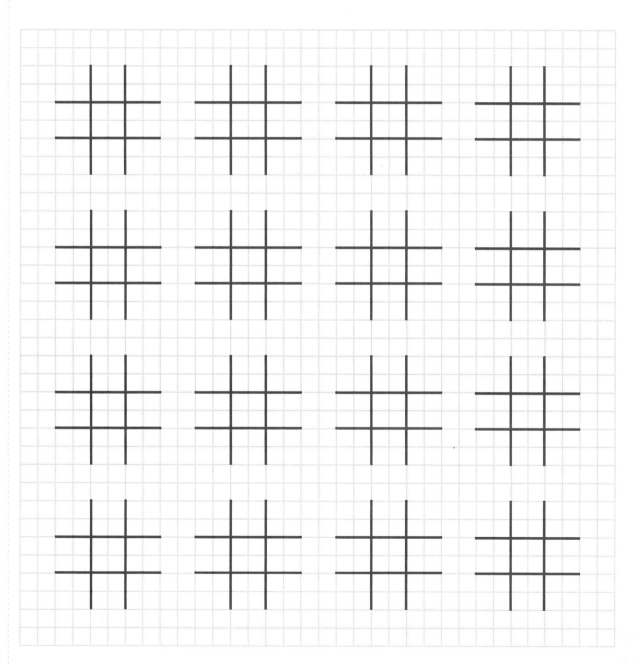

~ Noughts and Crosses ~

XOX

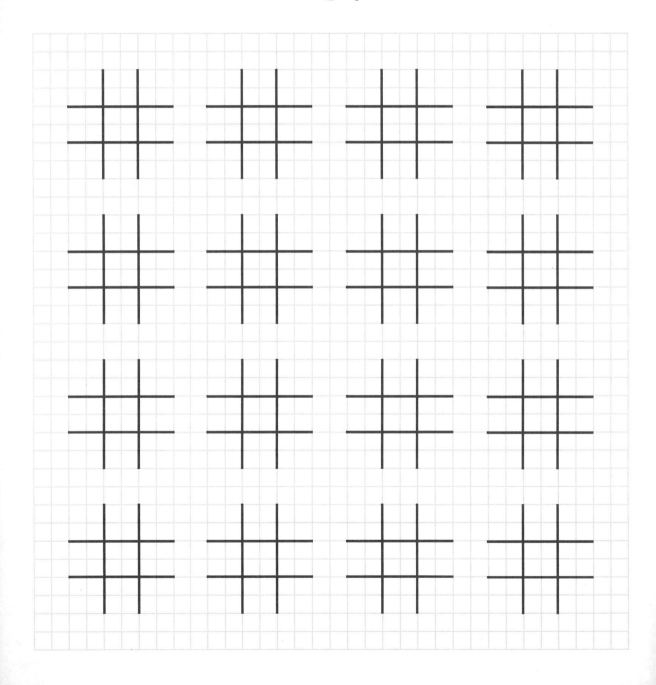

~ Noughts and Crosses ~

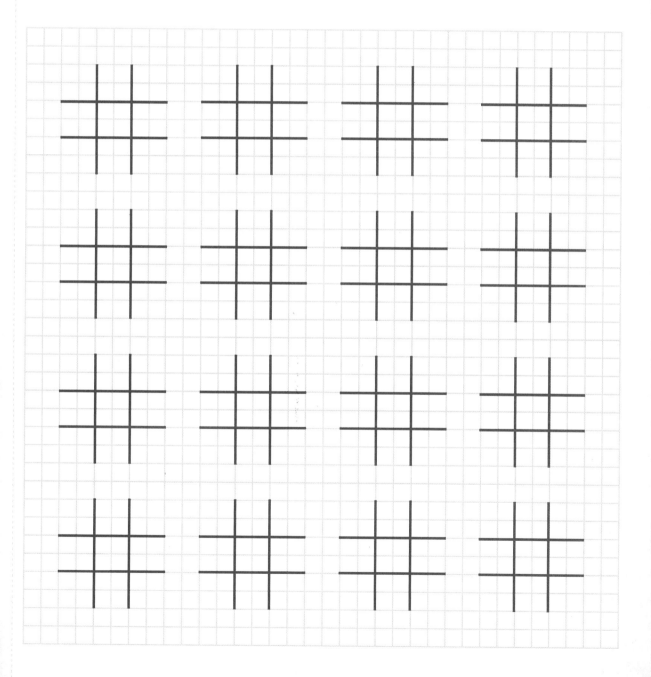

~ Noughts and Crosses ~

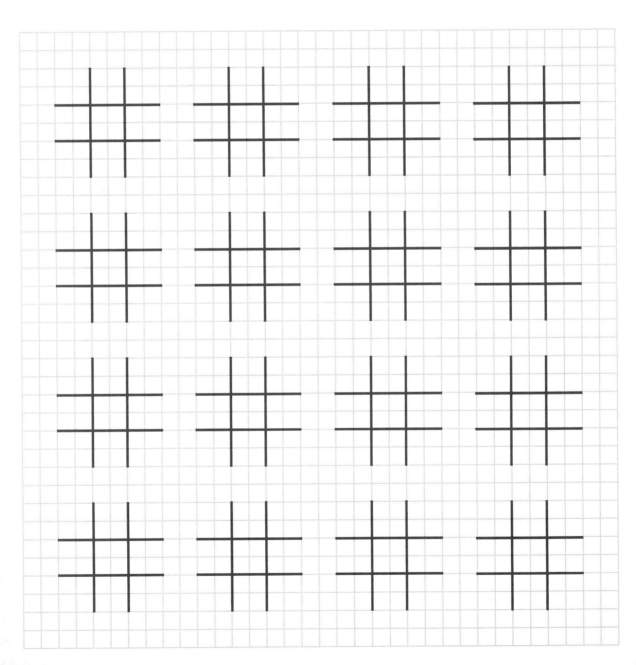

~ Noughts and Crosses ~

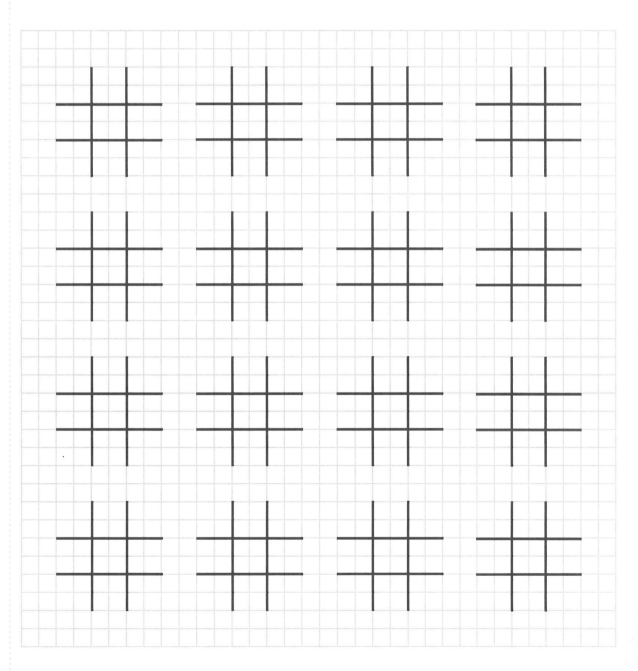

~ Noughts and Crosses ~

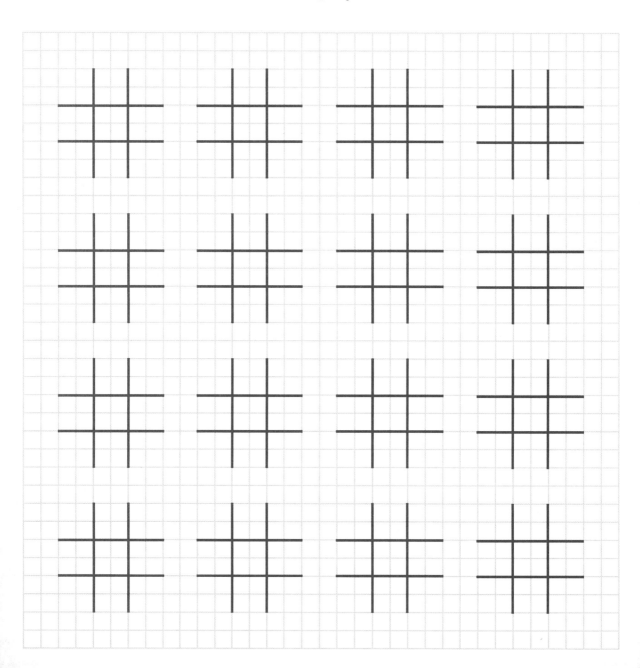

~ Noughts and Crosses ~

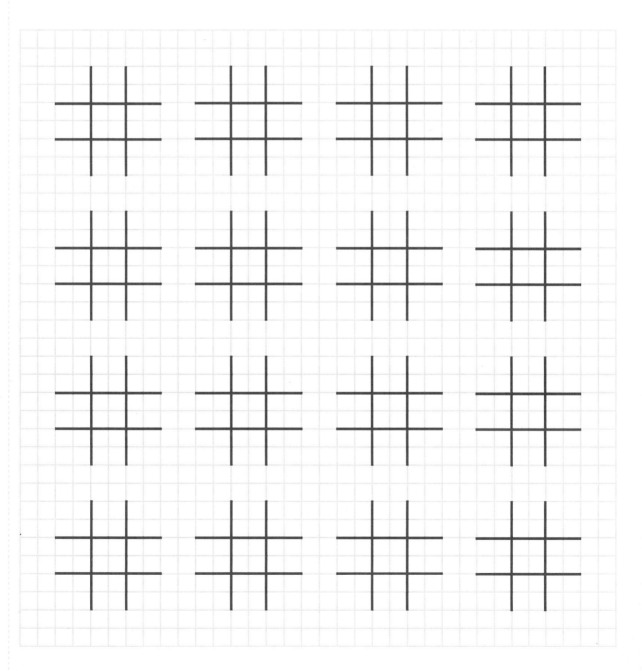

~ Noughts and Crosses ~

XOX

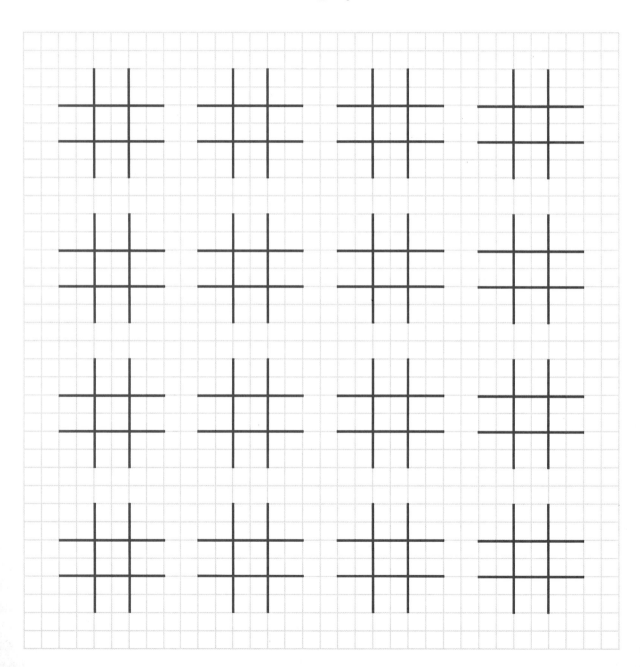

~ Noughts and Crosses ~

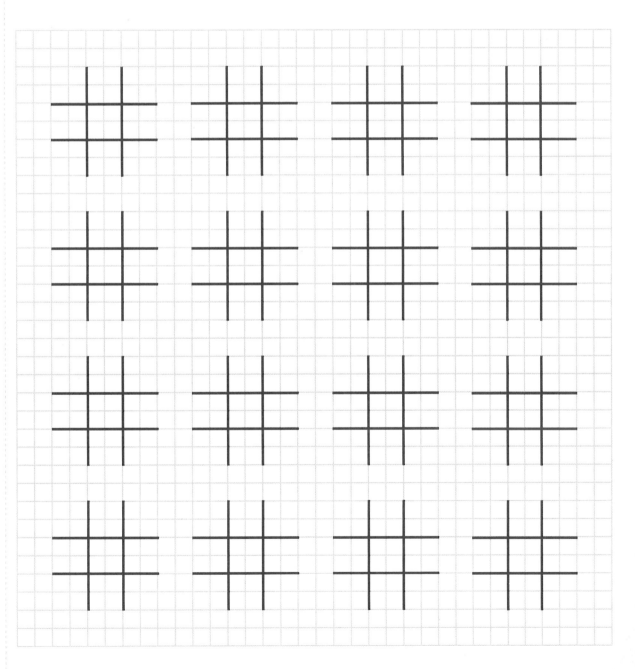

~ Noughts and Crosses ~

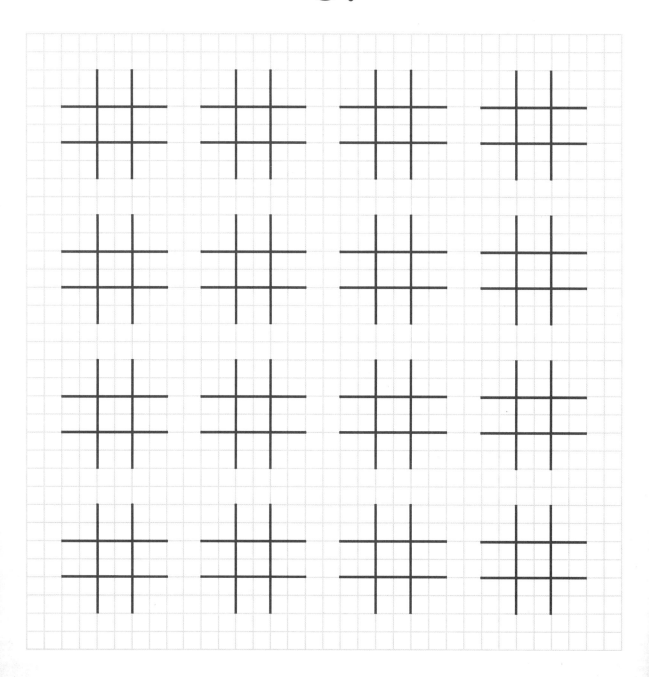

~ Noughts and Crosses ~

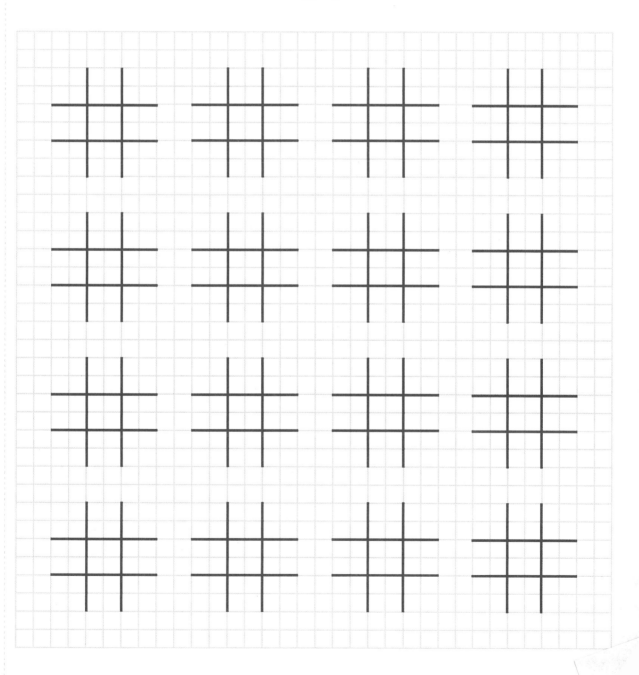

~ Super Noughts and Crosses ~

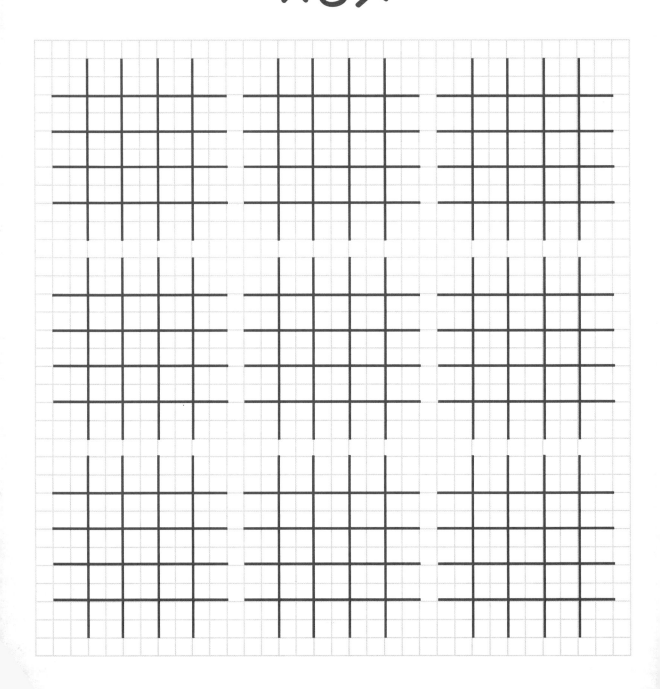

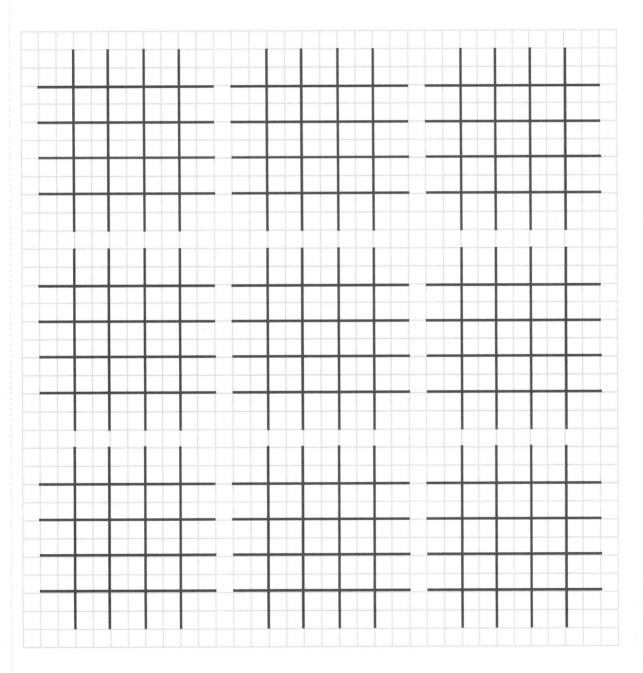

Super Noughts and Crosses

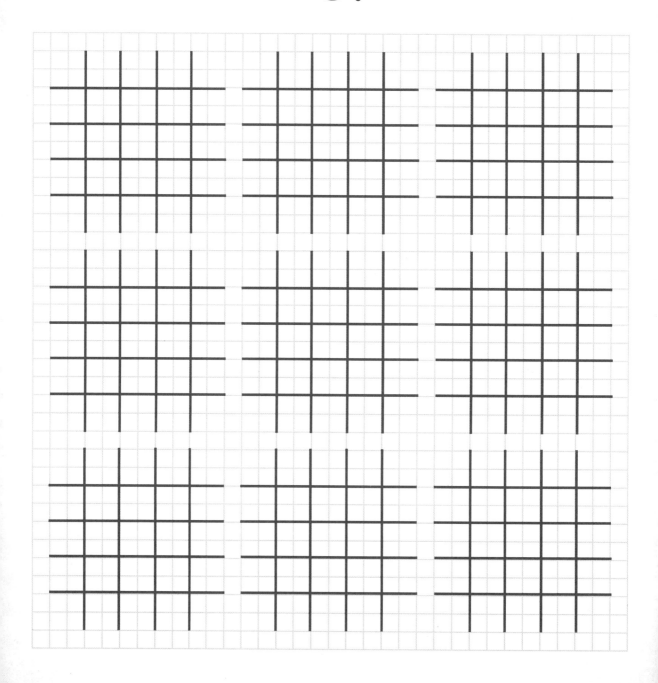

PAPER FORTUNE TELLER

The paper fortune teller was introduced in the origami book *Fun with Paper Folding*, published in America in 1928. Usually associated with Japan, the ancient art of paper folding was introduced by Buddhist monks from China in the sixth century. The shape was originally called a 'salt cellar' as the four open compartments could be used to hold salt and other condiments if it was placed standing on a table. Its use to snap at bugs provided one of its other nicknames: 'cootie catcher'.

Also known as a chatterbox or whirlybird, the fortune teller became a favourite with children, particularly in the 1950s and 60s. Instructions on how to make a fortune teller are overleaf.

HOW TO PLAY

- You need at least two players – the teller and the fortune seeker. Fortune tellers can also be used as a party game to provide forfeits.

- First, the seeker picks a colour. The teller spells out the colour by moving the fortune teller back and forth.

- Next, choose a number. Again, the teller counts out that number while manipulating the fortune teller open and closed.

- The seeker then picks a second number, and this time the flap is opened to reveal the fortune beneath.

TO MAKE THE FORTUNE TELLER

1. Take a square sheet of paper.

2. Fold the square corner to corner to create diagonal creases.

3. Fold the four corners into the centre to form the origami shape known as a 'cushion fold' or 'blintz base'. Turn over the smaller square that you have made.

4. Again, fold the four corners into the centre so the points meet in the middle. Write the numbers 1 through to 8 on the inner sections. Add the secret 'fortunes' under each flap. These can be an answer to a question, a prediction, dare, challenge or silly task – the choice is up to the creator

5. Flip the square over.

6. Fold the square horizontally and vertically.

7. Finally, tease out the flaps and work your index fingers and thumbs into the four pockets.

Manipulate the fortune teller by pulling and pinching, opening and closing it to keep two pairs of corners together and reveal only half the flaps at a time.

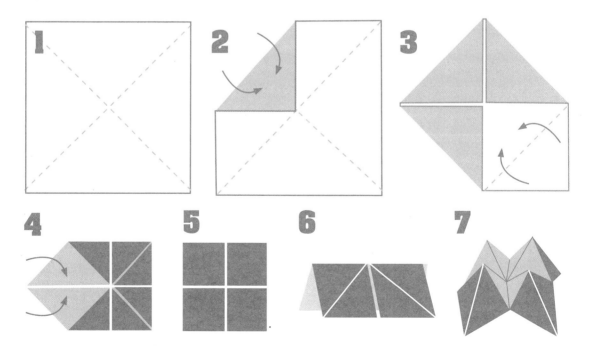

PAPER FORTUNE TELLER

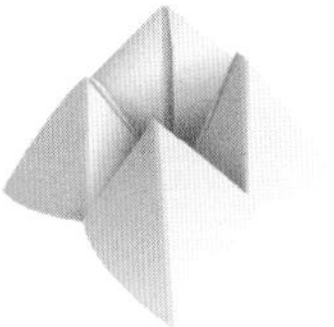

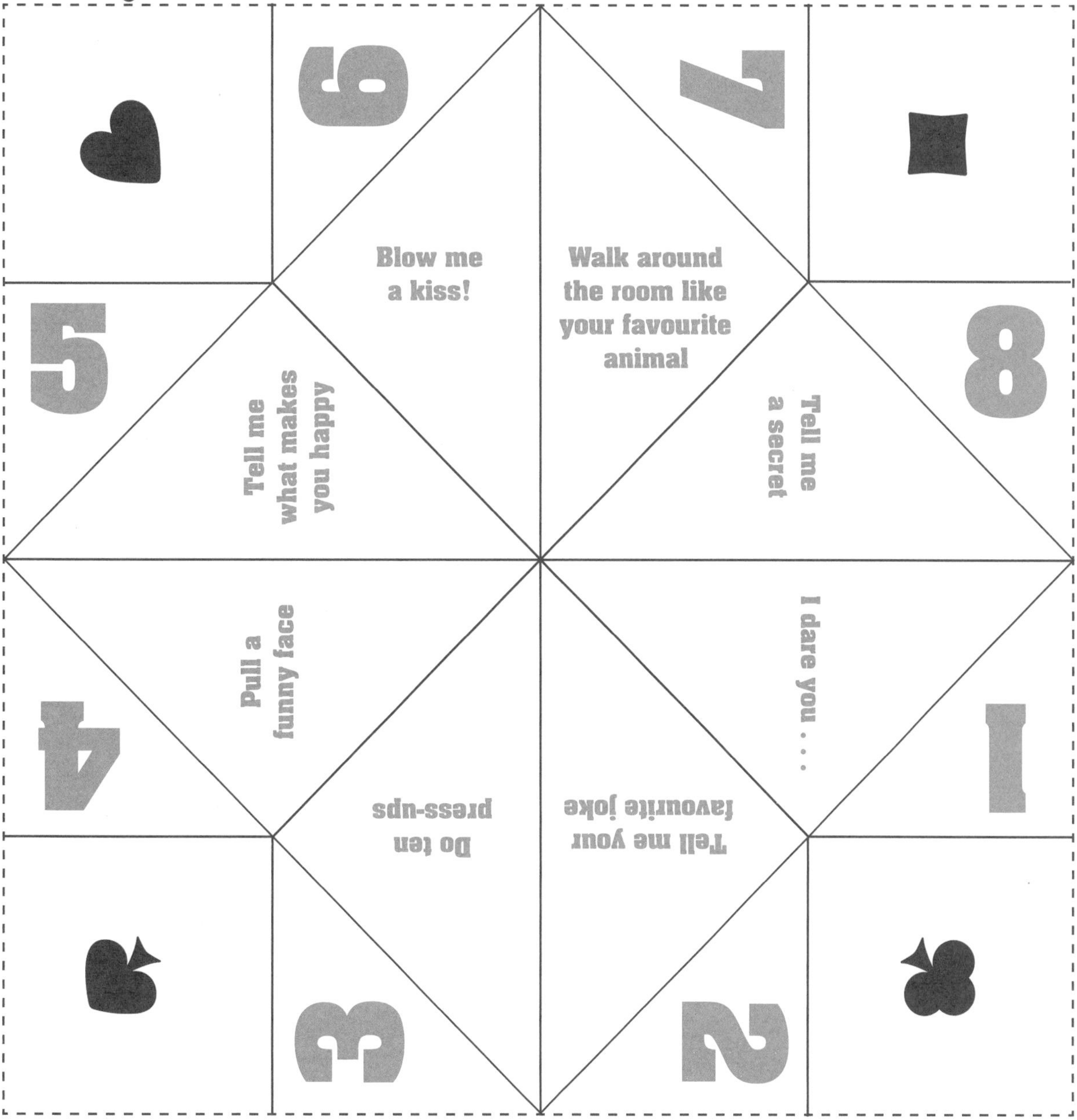

6

7

Blow me a kiss!

Walk around the room like your favourite animal

5

8

Tell me what makes you happy

Tell me a secret

Pull a funny face

I dare you . . . .

4

1

Do ten press-ups

Tell me your favourite joke

3

2

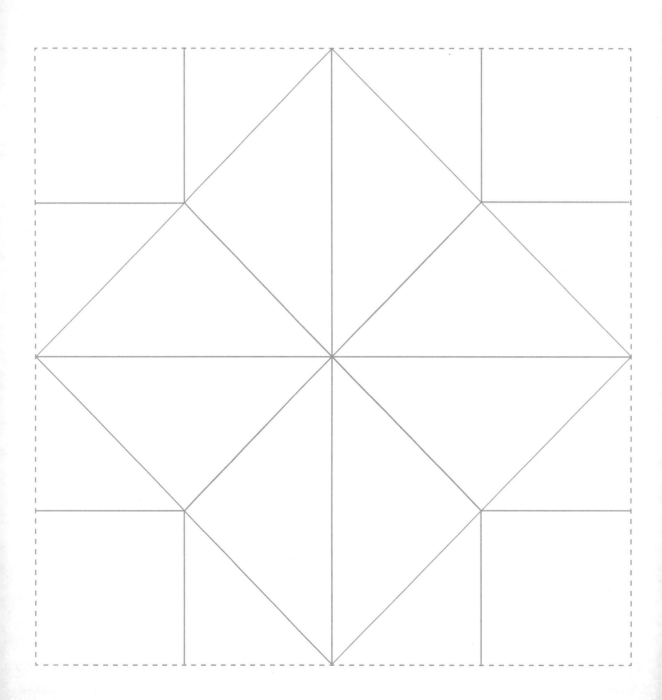

PAPER FORTUNE TELLER

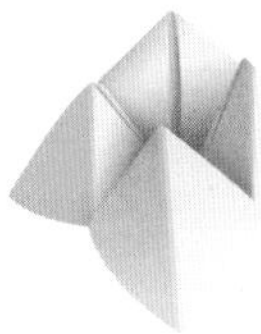

Touch your toes

Try to lick your elbow

Recite the alphabet backwards

Snort like a pig

Act out a death scene

Pull a silly face

Howl like a wolf

Count down from 100

6

7

5

8

4

1

3

2

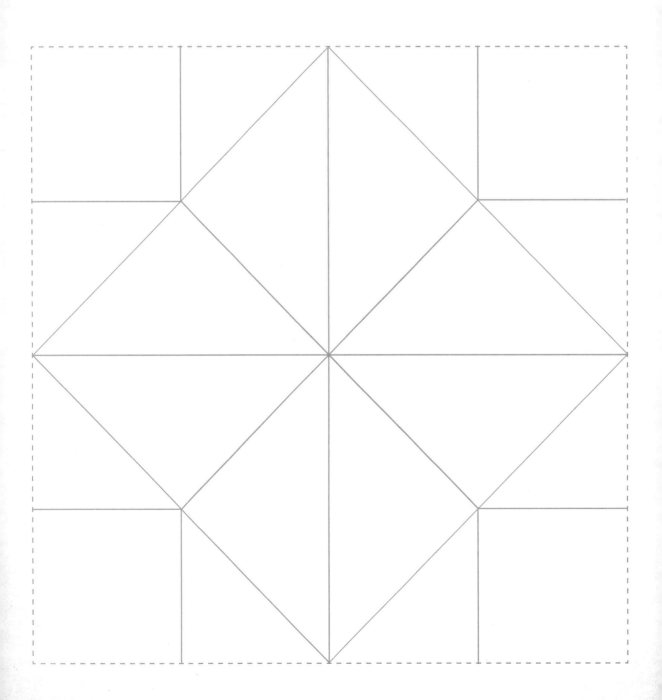

PAPER FORTUNE TELLER

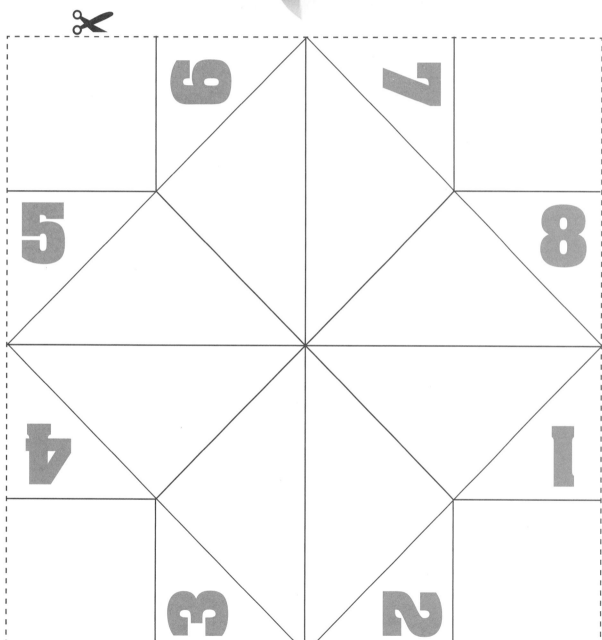

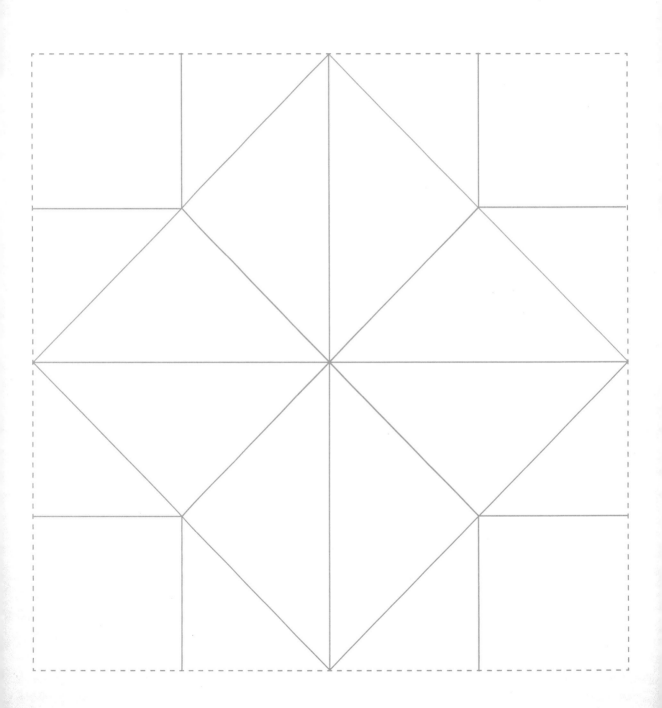

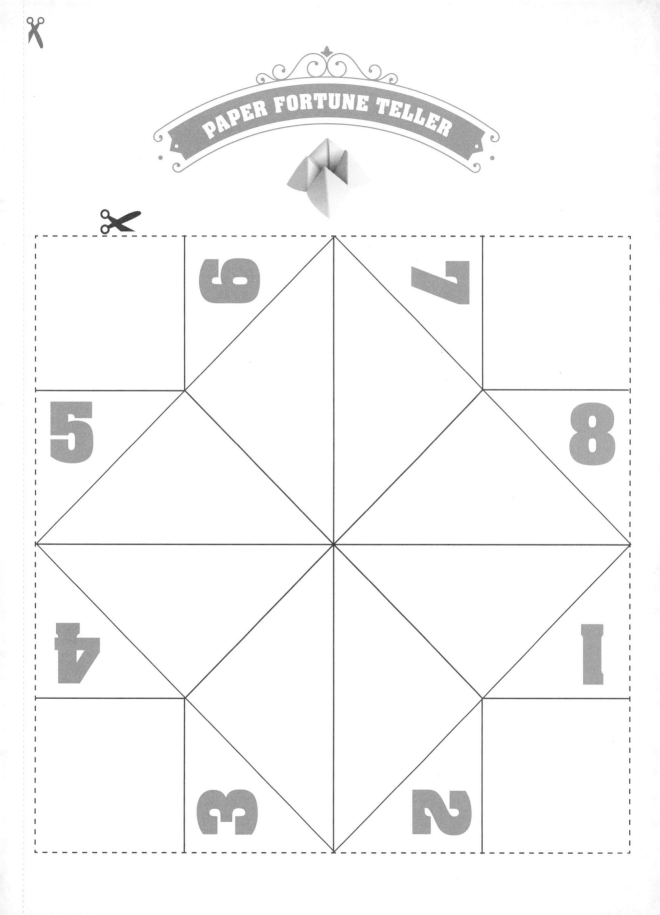

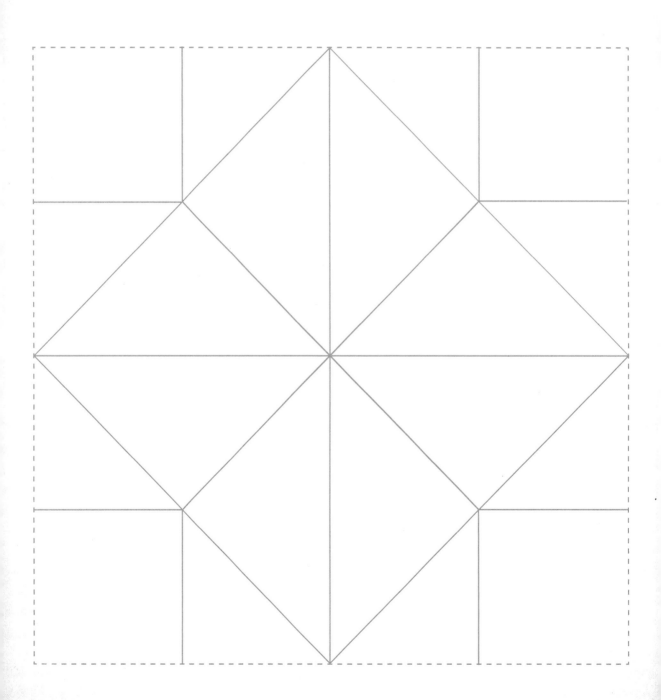

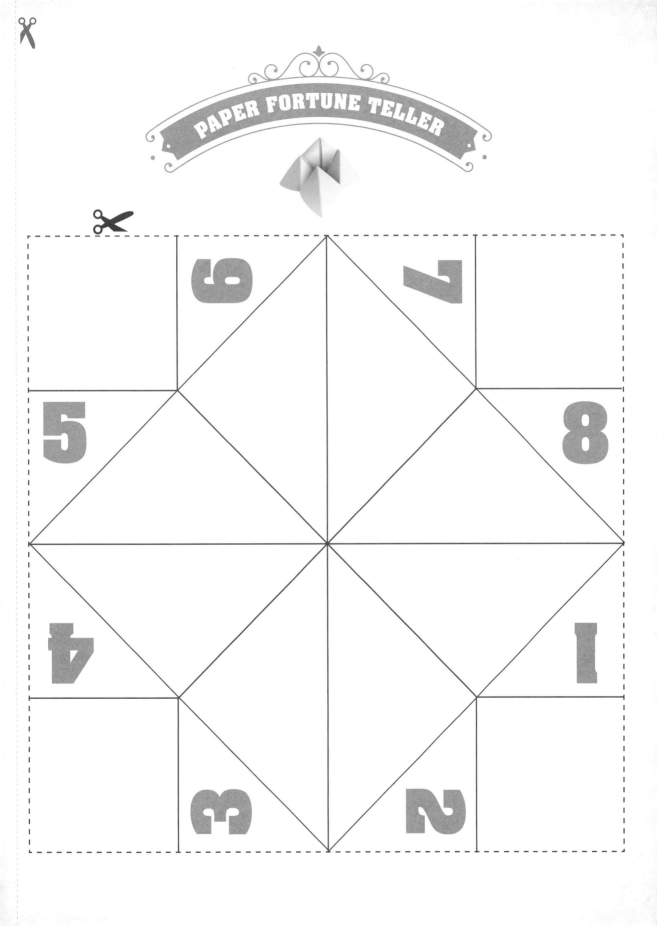

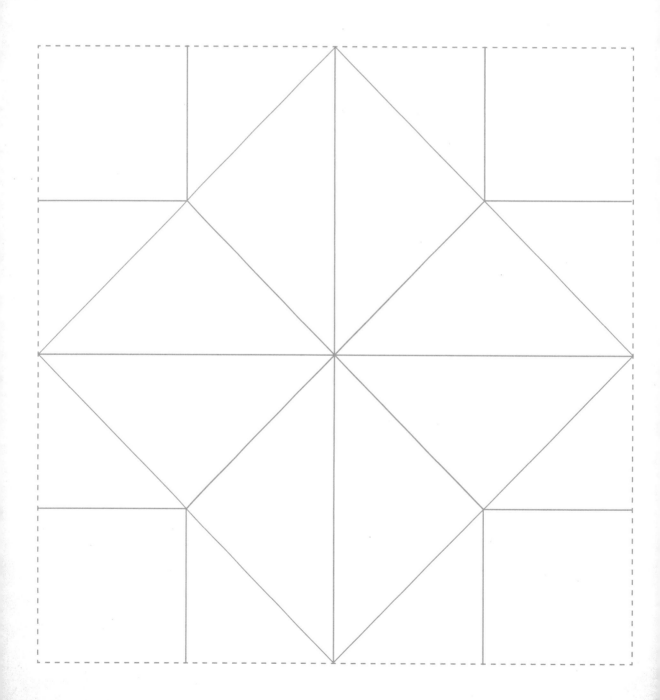

PAPER FORTUNE TELLER

6 7

5 8

4 1

3 2

Fortune ideas

You can be as creative and personal as you wish with your fortunes but here are some ideas to help get you started:

- Share a secret wish
- What annoys you most?
- What makes you sad?
- What makes you happy?
- What is the silliest thing you've ever done?
- What are you embarrassed by?
- What characteristic do you find most attractive?
- Life's too short for ...?

- You will meet a stranger
- Good news will arrive this week
- You'll get straight As
- You'll fall in love
- You'll catch a cold
- A surprise is in store for you
- A journey beckons
- Save your pennies

- **What's my mood?**
- Calm
- Hopeful
- Interested
- Bored
- Flirty
- Cheerful
- Grumpy
- Mad

- Take time to smell the flowers
- Never trouble trouble, till trouble troubles you
- Keep your friends close but your enemies closer
- Guard your secrets
- The road to riches is paved with homework
- An invitation is waiting for you
- Today is better than yesterday but not as good as tomorrow
- Ignore previous fortunes

- It could be better but it's good enough
- Be kind to animals
- Pick your friends with care and your nose in private
- You may soon have an out-of-money experience
- Whoever digs a hole will fall into it
- The wise see danger and take shelter. The foolish keep going and pay the penalty
- There's always a silver lining
- Two days from today, tomorrow will be yesterday

NINE MEN'S MORRIS

This ancient three-in-a-row game dates back at least to the Roman Empire. Boards have been discovered engraved on classical ruins and impressed into clay tiles. It has various names, including Mill, the Mill Game, Merrills, Merelles, Ninepenny Marl and Cowboy Checkers. A carved board was uncovered in a Viking burial ship excavated in Norway and it is likely that the Norse explorers spread the game throughout Europe, North Africa, Asia and perhaps even America on their voyages of discovery and conquest. The game is still played widely – in Norway it is known as *Mølle*, in Russia as *Melnitsa*, Germans call it *Mühle*, Italians *Mulinello* and Hungarians *Malom*. *Akidada* is a similar game played in Nigeria. It has sometimes been suggested that the name may come from Morris (or Moorish) dances but it is more likely to have its origins in the Latin word for a gaming counter, *merellus*.

In medieval England, Morris games were played during fairs and pageants with girls and boys acting as the living counters. The Morris board was marked out on the ground and the game players would tell their live pieces where to move. Titania refers to such a game in Shakespeare's *A Midsummer Night's Dream*. Boards can also be found carved on the cloister seats of many notable English cathedrals including Canterbury, Salisbury and Westminster Abbey. The Pilgrim Fathers took the game with them when they settled in America, where it remained a popular pastime for soldiers during the Civil War.

RULES OF THE GAME

- Two players with nine counters or 'men' apiece. Use different colours or types of counter for each player – small coins, buttons or beans work well if you don't have counters.

- The players decide who will go first and then take turns placing one counter at a time on the dots on the board.

- The aim is to make a row of three 'men' along any straight line, vertically or horizontally. A row of three is called a 'mill'.

- When a player has formed a mill, he may take one of his opponent's men from the board.

- Once all the counters are in position, players take turns moving one counter to the next empty point. Jumping over another counter is strictly forbidden at this stage of the game.

- When a player has only three counters left, he is allowed to 'fly' or jump to any vacant point; the rule that he may only move to adjacent points is lifted.

- You may not remove a counter from another player's mill unless he has no other counters on the board.

- Any captured counters are out of the game.

Winners and losers

The loser is the first player to be reduced to two pieces, making a row of three impossible, or the first to be blocked from moving.

 TIPS

In the opening stage, spread your counters across the board, making it harder for your opponent to block you. Position your counters to make it possible to move them in several directions. Ideally, place three counters to allow you to move one back and forward to open and close a mill, bearing in mind you capture one of your opponent's counters every time you close a mill.

Nine Men's Morris is the most popular of the Morris games but there are variations referring to the number of counters each player uses in a game.

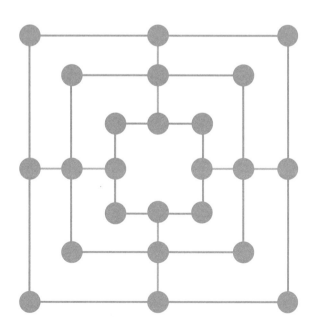

SIX MEN'S MORRIS

This version was very popular across medieval Europe but seems to have fallen out of favour at the beginning of the seventeenth century. The board is smaller than that used for Nine Men's Morris as it does not have the outer square. It is a good preparation for playing the more challenging Nine Men game. Seven Men's Morris, played with fourteen counters in total, uses the same board but with a cross in the middle.

RULES OF THE GAME

- Two players each have six counters.

- The rules of the game are the same as those for Nine Men's Morris but 'flying' is not allowed at any stage of the game.

- The loser is again the first player to have only two counters left on the board, or who is blocked from moving.

THREE MEN'S MORRIS

The three-men version of a Morris game can be played on the three-square grid used in noughts and crosses or using the points of a two-square grid. The rules are slightly different from the Six and Nine Men games.

RULES OF THE GAME

- Two players each have three counters.

- Players take turns placing one counter at a time on the board for their first three turns.

- A player wins if a row of three, or mill, is formed during these rounds, otherwise play continues.

- Players carry on taking turns moving one of their counters to either any empty position, or any empty adjacent position. Players should decide beforehand which of the two game rules they are following.

- The winner is the first player to form a mill.

NINE MEN'S MORRIS

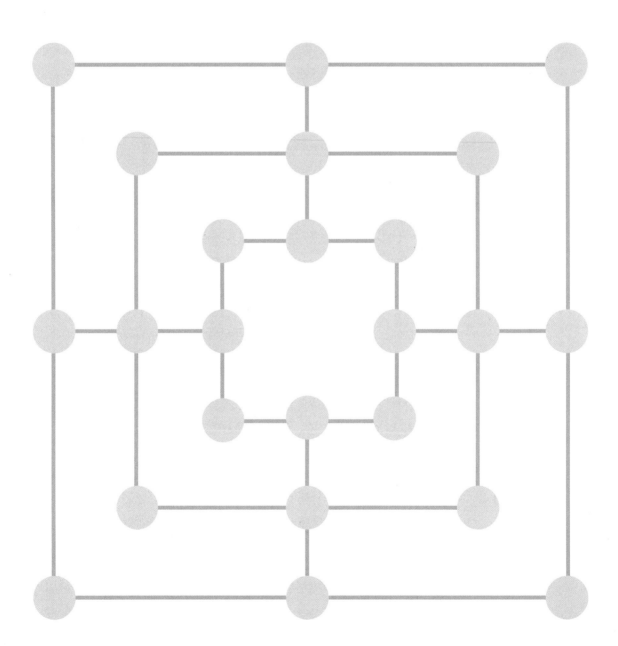

NINE MEN'S MORRIS

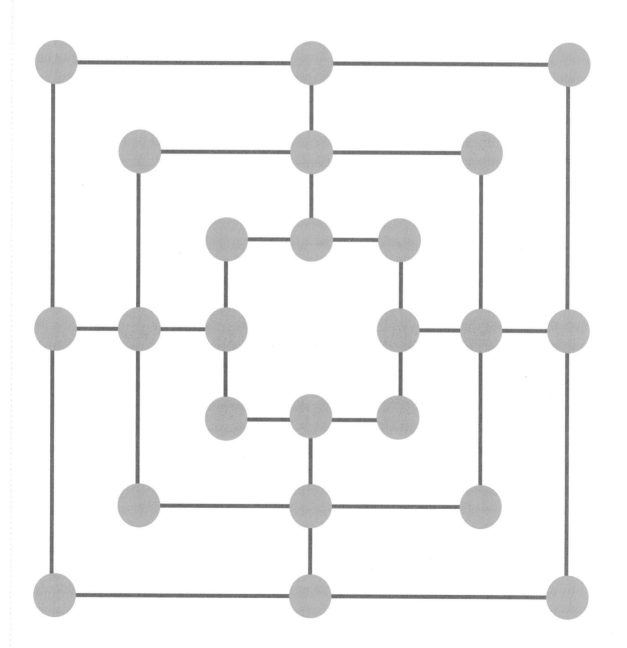

SIX MEN'S MORRIS

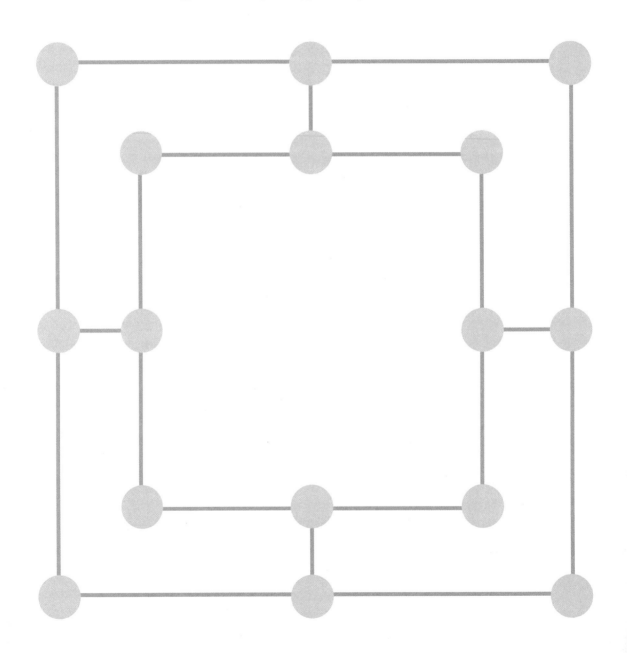

SIX MEN'S MORRIS

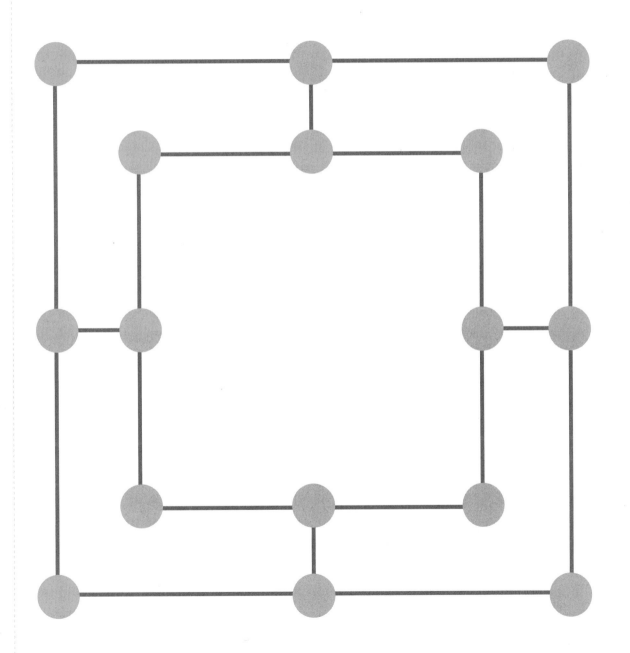

THREE MEN'S MORRIS

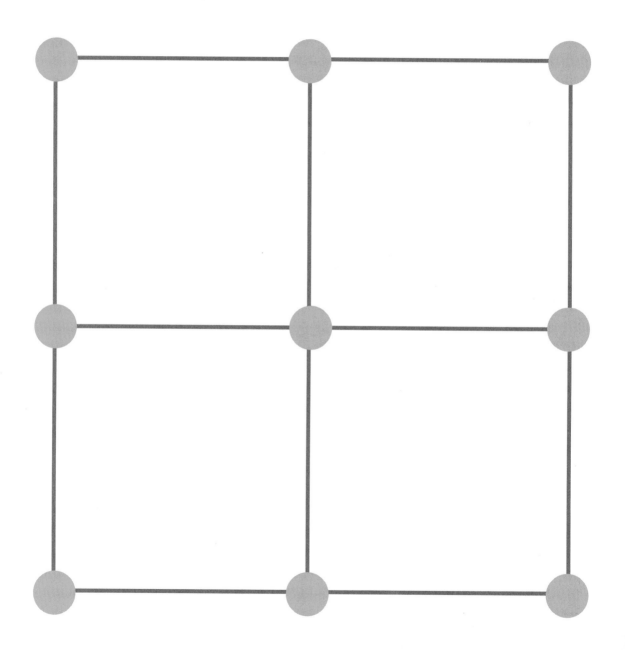

THREE MEN'S MORRIS

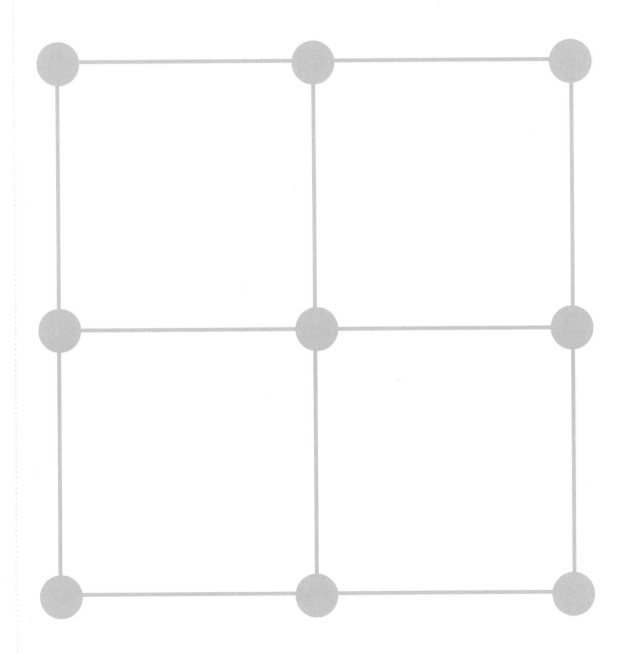

THREE MEN'S MORRIS

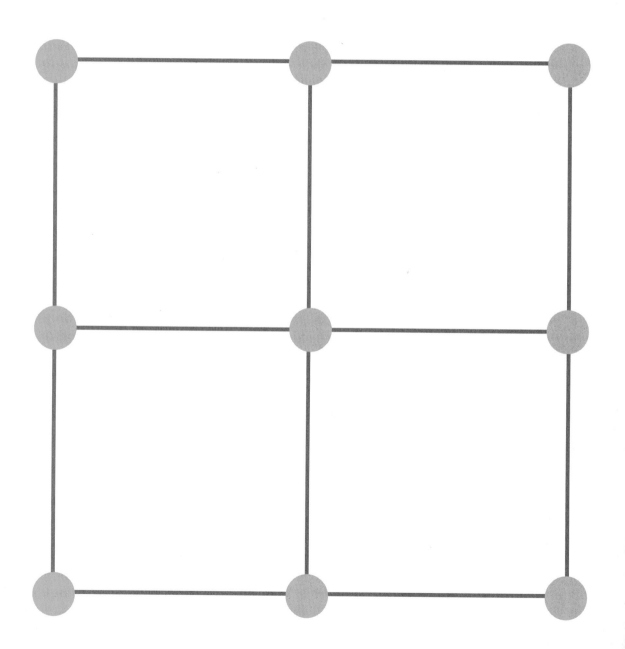

BULLS AND COWS

There are many names for what is essentially a code-breaking game for two or more players. It is sometimes known as Bulls and Cleots, or Pigs and Bulls, and is really the same as the board game 'Master Mind'. It has been played for at least the last century and probably a lot longer.

The desire for privacy and need to hide the true message means that man has been writing in code for almost as long as people have been writing as a means of communication. Almost two thousand years ago, Julius Caesar used a simple shift code to confuse enemies when sending details of tactics and battle plans to his commanders. Since then, secret codes have famously hidden plots, conspiracies and invasions, from Mary Queen of Scots' ciphered messages to Babington scheming to assassinate Queen Elizabeth, through to Renaissance rulers and Allied and Axis powers' use of codes during World War II.

RULES OF THE GAME

The game is most often played by two opponents but it can also be played by two teams of two to three players.

- Player One writes down a secret four-digit code. Numbers chosen must be between one and six, and each number in the code must be different. The code is covered and kept hidden.
- Player Two then makes their first attempt at guessing the code.
- Player One marks any matches. Numbers that are correct and in the right position are marked as 'bulls' and any numbers that match but are in the wrong position are 'cows'. Numbers can be either cows or bulls; they can't be both.
- The aim is to crack the code in as few attempts as possible.
- The game can be made more competitive if both players or teams set codes at the same time, with each trying to beat the opposition to break the code first and win the round.

SECRET NUMBER	2516	COWS	BULLS
GUESS 1	1234	2	0
GUESS 2	4326	1	1
GUESS 3	4512	1	2
GUESS 4	2156	2	2
GUESS 5	6152	4	0
GUESS 6	2516	0	4

BULLS AND COWS

SECRET NUMBER		COWS	BULLS
GUESS 1			
GUESS 2			
GUESS 3			
GUESS 4			
GUESS 5			
GUESS 6			

SECRET NUMBER		COWS	BULLS
GUESS 1			
GUESS 2			
GUESS 3			
GUESS 4			
GUESS 5			
GUESS 6			

BULLS AND COWS

SECRET NUMBER		COWS	BULLS
GUESS 1			
GUESS 2			
GUESS 3			
GUESS 4			
GUESS 5			
GUESS 6			

SECRET NUMBER		COWS	BULLS
GUESS 1			
GUESS 2			
GUESS 3			
GUESS 4			
GUESS 5			
GUESS 6			

BULLS AND COWS

SECRET NUMBER		COWS	BULLS
GUESS 1			
GUESS 2			
GUESS 3			
GUESS 4			
GUESS 5			
GUESS 6			

SECRET NUMBER		COWS	BULLS
GUESS 1			
GUESS 2			
GUESS 3			
GUESS 4			
GUESS 5			
GUESS 6			

BULLS AND COWS

SECRET NUMBER		COWS	BULLS
GUESS 1			
GUESS 2			
GUESS 3			
GUESS 4			
GUESS 5			
GUESS 6			

SECRET NUMBER		COWS	BULLS
GUESS 1			
GUESS 2			
GUESS 3			
GUESS 4			
GUESS 5			
GUESS 6			

BULLS AND COWS

SECRET NUMBER		COWS	BULLS
GUESS 1			
GUESS 2			
GUESS 3			
GUESS 4			
GUESS 5			
GUESS 6			

SECRET NUMBER		COWS	BULLS
GUESS 1			
GUESS 2			
GUESS 3			
GUESS 4			
GUESS 5			
GUESS 6			

BULLS AND COWS

SECRET NUMBER		COWS	BULLS
GUESS 1			
GUESS 2			
GUESS 3			
GUESS 4			
GUESS 5			
GUESS 6			

SECRET NUMBER		COWS	BULLS
GUESS 1			
GUESS 2			
GUESS 3			
GUESS 4			
GUESS 5			
GUESS 6			

BULLS AND COWS

SECRET NUMBER		COWS	BULLS
GUESS 1			
GUESS 2			
GUESS 3			
GUESS 4			
GUESS 5			
GUESS 6			

SECRET NUMBER		COWS	BULLS
GUESS 1			
GUESS 2			
GUESS 3			
GUESS 4			
GUESS 5			
GUESS 6			

BULLS AND COWS

SECRET NUMBER		COWS	BULLS
GUESS 1			
GUESS 2			
GUESS 3			
GUESS 4			
GUESS 5			
GUESS 6			

SECRET NUMBER		COWS	BULLS
GUESS 1			
GUESS 2			
GUESS 3			
GUESS 4			
GUESS 5			
GUESS 6			

BULLS AND COWS

SECRET NUMBER		COWS	BULLS
GUESS 1			
GUESS 2			
GUESS 3			
GUESS 4			
GUESS 5			
GUESS 6			

SECRET NUMBER		COWS	BULLS
GUESS 1			
GUESS 2			
GUESS 3			
GUESS 4			
GUESS 5			
GUESS 6			

BULLS AND COWS

SECRET NUMBER		COWS	BULLS
GUESS 1			
GUESS 2			
GUESS 3			
GUESS 4			
GUESS 5			
GUESS 6			

SECRET NUMBER		COWS	BULLS
GUESS 1			
GUESS 2			
GUESS 3			
GUESS 4			
GUESS 5			
GUESS 6			

DOTS
AND
BOXES

Unlike most traditional pencil and paper games where the origins are slightly obscure, the description of Dots and Boxes was first published in 1889 by the French mathematician Edouard Lucas. His name for it was 'La Pipopipette' and it is sometimes known as Pigs in a Pen, along with simply Boxes, Dots or Dot to Dot.

Whatever the name, the aim is basically to join the dots and complete as many boxes as possible. It can be played very simply on a two-square grid but the five-square version is more popular as it makes for a more satisfying contest. Seven-, eight- and nine-square grids can all be used; the bigger the grid the greater the challenge and longer the game lasts. Versions of the game are played across the world from South America through Scandinavia and Europe.

RULES OF THE GAME

- This is a game for two players.

- Player One joins any two dots anywhere on the grid with a horizontal or vertical line.

- Player Two follows suit.

- Players take turns drawing lines. When a player adds the line that completes a box, he is awarded an extra turn and claims the box by writing his initial inside.

- The game ends when the grid is complete and no more lines can be drawn.

- The winner is the player who has made the most boxes.

☞ **TIPS**

Play usually begins with a fairly random set of lines, as the main goal should be to avoid adding the third side of a box. When all the potential boxes are joined into a long chain, the last player has an advantage as they are able to close all the boxes in the chain. The player that opens a long chain usually loses the game.

FIVE-SQUARED

GAME 1

GAME 2

GAME 3

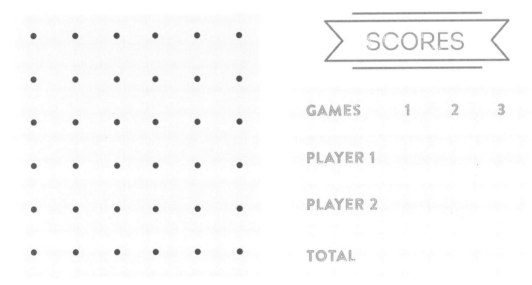

GAMES	1	2	3
PLAYER 1			
PLAYER 2			
TOTAL			

SCORES

FIVE-SQUARED

GAME 1

GAME 2

GAME 3

SCORES

GAMES	1	2	3
PLAYER 1			
PLAYER 2			
TOTAL			

FIVE-SQUARED

GAME 1

GAME 2

GAME 3

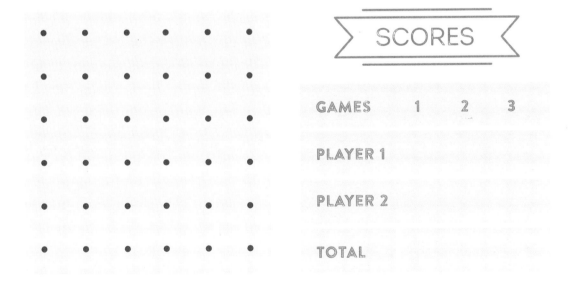

SCORES

GAMES	1	2	3
PLAYER 1			
PLAYER 2			
TOTAL			

SEVEN-SQUARED

GAME 1

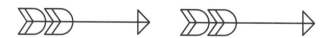

SEVEN-SQUARED

GAME 2

GAMES	1	2	TOTAL
PLAYER 1			
PLAYER 2			

EIGHT-SQUARED

GAME 1

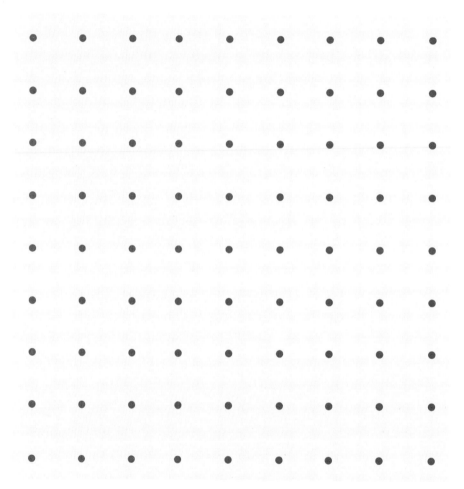

EIGHT-SQUARED

GAME 2

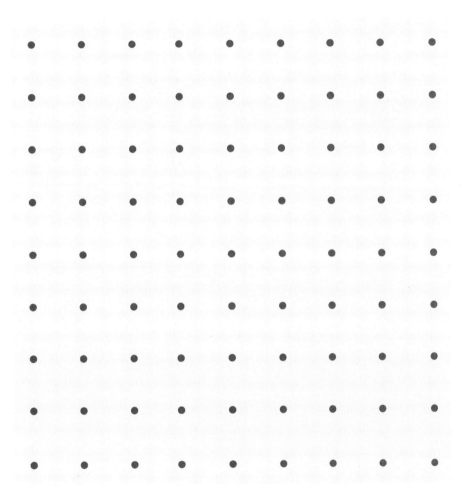

SCORES	GAMES	1	2	TOTAL
	PLAYER 1			
	PLAYER 2			

NINE-SQUARED

GAME 1

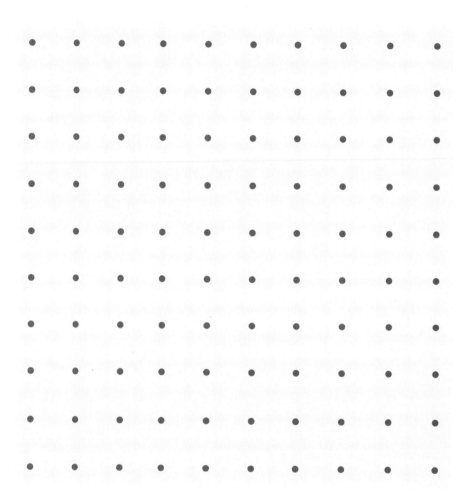

NINE-SQUARED

GAME 2

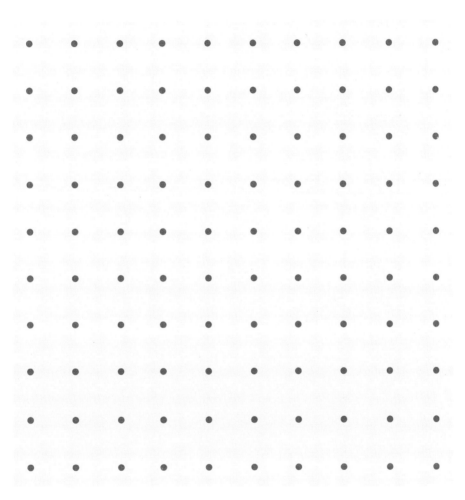

NINE-SQUARED

GAME 3

GAMES	1	2	3	TOTAL
PLAYER 1				
PLAYER 2				